JSCRIPT SOURCE CODE: WBEMSCRIPTING EXECNOTIFICATIONQUERY ASYNC

__InstanceModificationEvent

Richard Edwards

WELCOME TO THE WORLD OF MANAGEMENT CODE

Or how about just hello?

I can't think of a better time than now to either learn something about a new language or take the rust off those genus brain cells of yours. Either way, this book will give you the code you need to know to do one thing right: Use Javascript with Winmgmts and use get to get your way with WMI. There will be source code books on InstancesOf, ExecQuery and ExecNotificationQuery, too. And, there will be the Async versions, as well.

Also, some words of caution. Don't buy the Jscript version because it is exactly the same. Also, because Amazon won't let me wrap this up in 25 pages, you are going to see the same sample code over and over again.

Not that the sample code is boring, you shouldn't have to buy it more than once.

WHAT YOU SHOULD EXPECT FROM ME

WHAT YOU SHOULDN'T EXPECT FROM ME

WHAT YOU WILL GET FROM ME

Lots of code. Fact is, there will be over 100 pages of code you can use.

And with that said, let's cover some of the core concepts we're going to be using in this book

There are roughly 12 building blocks here:

- var ws = new ActiveXObject("WScript.Shell");
- var Names = new ActiveXObject("Scripting.Dictionary");
- var Col = new ActiveXObject("Scripting.Dictionary");
- var Rows = new ActiveXObject("Scripting.Dictionary");
- var fso = new ActiveXObject("Scripting.FileSystemObject");
- var oExcel = new ActiveXObject("Excel.Application");

DECLARATIONS

I like my declarations at the very top of my scripts. So, it is common to see:

```
var x = 0;
var y = 0;
var v = 0;

var svc = null;
var ob = null;
var objs = null;

var sink = null;

var Orientation = "Multi-Line Horizontal";

var Names = new ActiveXObject("Scripting.Dictionary");
var Rows = new ActiveXObject("Scripting.Dictionary");

var txtstream=null;
```

Notice that I put a space between the groups I will be using in various places in my code.

INITIALIZATION CODE

Because we aren't doing anything fancy here, the initialization code is pretty much straight forward:

```
var x = 0;
var y = 0;
var v = 0;

var svc = null;
var ob = null;
var objs = null;

var sink = null;

var Orientation = "Multi-Line Horizontal";

var Names = new ActiveXObject("Scripting.Dictionary");
var Rows = new ActiveXObject("Scripting.Dictionary");

var txtstream=null;

function sink_OnObjectReady(objWbemObject, objWbemAsyncContext)
{
   if(y==5)
   {
      v=1;
      sink.Cancel();
      return;
   }
   var obj = objWbemObject.Properties_.Item("TargetInstance").Value;
   var propset = obj.properties_;
```

```
var propEnum = new Enumerator(propset);
var Cols = new ActiveXObject("Scripting.Dictionary");
for (; !propEnum.atEnd(); propEnum.moveNext())
{
   var  prop = propEnum.item();
   if(y==0)
   {
      Names.Add(x, prop.name);
   }
   Cols.Add(x, GetValue(prop.name, obj));
   x=x+1;
}
x=0;
Rows.Add(y, Cols);
y=y+1;
}


var l = new ActiveXObject("WbemScripting.SWbemLocator");
var svc = l.ConnectServer(".", "root\\cimv2");
svc.Security_.AuthenticationLevel = 6;
svc.Security_.ImpersonationLevel = 3;
sink = WScript.CreateObject("WbemScripting.SWbemSink", "sink_");
svc.ExecNotificationQueryAsync(sink, "Select * from ___InstanceModificationEvent
within 1 where TargetInstance ISA 'Win32_Process'");

while(v ==0)
{
   WScript.Sleep(500);
}
```

GETVALUE CODE

To make working with the code much easier to deal with than having to deal with each datatype WbemScripting can throw at you.

```
function GetValue(Name, obj)
{
  var tempstr = new String();
  var tempstr1 = new String();
  var tName = new String();
  tempstr1 = obj.GetObjectText_();
  var re = /"/g;
  tempstr1 = tempstr1.replace(re , "");
  var pos;
  tName = Name + " = ";
  pos = tempstr1.indexOf(tName);
  if (pos > -1)
  {
    pos = pos + tName.length;
    tempstr = tempstr1.substring(pos, tempstr1.length);
    pos = tempstr.indexOf(";");
    tempstr = tempstr.substring(0, pos);
    tempstr = tempstr.replace("{", "");
    tempstr = tempstr.replace("}", "");
    if (tempstr.length > 13)
    {
      if (obj.Properties_(Name).CIMType == 101)
      {
```

```
                tempstr = tempstr.substr(4, 2) + "/"  + tempstr.substr(6, 2) + "/" +
tempstr.substr(0, 3) + " " + tempstr.substr(8, 2) + ":" + tempstr.substr(10, 2) + ":" +
tempstr.substr(12, 2);
                }
            }
            return tempstr;
        }
        else
        {
            return "";
        }
    }
```

PUTTING IT ALL TOGETHER

So, let's put all of this together. The good news, you only have to do this once. How so?

Well, once you have the names and columns and rows populated, the rest of the coding examples can be used no matter what kind of coding you're doing with WbemScripting.

```javascript
var x = 0;
var y = 0;
var v = 0;

var svc = null;
var ob = null;
var objs = null;

var sink = null;

var Orientation = "Multi-Line Horizontal";

var Names = new ActiveXObject("Scripting.Dictionary");
var Rows = new ActiveXObject("Scripting.Dictionary");

var txtstream=null;

function sink_OnObjectReady(objWbemObject, objWbemAsyncContext)
{
   if(y==5)
   {
      v=1;
```

```
      sink.Cancel();
      return;
   }
   var obj = objWbemObject.Properties_.Item("TargetInstance").Value;
   var propset = obj.properties_;
   var propEnum = new Enumerator(propset);
   var Cols = new ActiveXObject("Scripting.Dictionary");
   for (; !propEnum.atEnd(); propEnum.moveNext())
   {
      var  prop = propEnum.item();
      if(y==0)
      {
         Names.Add(x, prop.name);
      }
      Cols.Add(x, GetValue(prop.name, obj));
      x=x+1;
   }
   x=0;
   Rows.Add(y, Cols);
   y=y+1;
}

var l = new ActiveXObject("WbemScripting.SWbemLocator");
var svc = l.ConnectServer(".", "root\\cimv2");
svc.Security_.AuthenticationLevel = 6;
svc.Security_.ImpersonationLevel = 3;
sink = WScript.CreateObject("WbemScripting.SWbemSink", "sink_");
svc.ExecNotificationQueryAsync(sink, "Select * from ___InstanceModificationEvent
within 1 where TargetInstance ISA 'Win32_Process'");

while(v ==0)
{
   WScript.Sleep(500);
}

var ws = new ActiveXObject("WScript.Shell");
var fso = new ActiveXObject("Scripting.FileSystemObject");
txtstream = fso.OpenTextFile(ws.CurrentDirectory + "\\Process.html", 2, true, -2);
txtstream.WriteLine("<html>");
txtstream.WriteLine("<head>");
```

```
txtstream.WriteLine("<title>Win32_Process</title>");
txtstream.WriteLine("<style type='text/css'>");
txtstream.WriteLine("body");
txtstream.WriteLine("{");
txtstream.WriteLine("    PADDING-RIGHT: 0px;");
txtstream.WriteLine("    PADDING-LEFT: 0px;");
txtstream.WriteLine("    PADDING-BOTTOM: 0px;");
txtstream.WriteLine("    MARGIN: 0px;");
txtstream.WriteLine("    COLOR: #333;");
txtstream.WriteLine("    PADDING-TOP: 0px;");
txtstream.WriteLine("    FONT-FAMILY: verdana, arial, helvetica, sans-serif;");
txtstream.WriteLine("}");
txtstream.WriteLine("table");
txtstream.WriteLine("{");
txtstream.WriteLine("    BORDER-RIGHT: #999999 1px solid;");
txtstream.WriteLine("    PADDING-RIGHT: 1px;");
txtstream.WriteLine("    PADDING-LEFT: 1px;");
txtstream.WriteLine("    PADDING-BOTTOM: 1px;");
txtstream.WriteLine("    LINE-HEIGHT: 8px;");
txtstream.WriteLine("    PADDING-TOP: 1px;");
txtstream.WriteLine("    BORDER-BOTTOM: #999 1px solid;");
txtstream.WriteLine("    BACKGROUND-COLOR: #eeeeee;");
txtstream.WriteLine("
filter:progid:DXImageTransform.Microsoft.Shadow(color='silver',     Direction=135,
Strength=16)");
txtstream.WriteLine("}");
txtstream.WriteLine("th");
txtstream.WriteLine("{");
txtstream.WriteLine("    BORDER-RIGHT: #999999 3px solid;");
txtstream.WriteLine("    PADDING-RIGHT: 6px;");
txtstream.WriteLine("    PADDING-LEFT: 6px;");
txtstream.WriteLine("    FONT-WEIGHT: Bold;");
txtstream.WriteLine("    FONT-SIZE: 14px;");
txtstream.WriteLine("    PADDING-BOTTOM: 6px;");
txtstream.WriteLine("    COLOR: darkred;");
txtstream.WriteLine("    LINE-HEIGHT: 14px;");
txtstream.WriteLine("    PADDING-TOP: 6px;");
txtstream.WriteLine("    BORDER-BOTTOM: #999 1px solid;");
txtstream.WriteLine("    BACKGROUND-COLOR: #eeeeee;");
txtstream.WriteLine("    FONT-FAMILY: font-family: Cambria, serif;");
```

```
txtstream.WriteLine("    FONT-SIZE: 12px;");
txtstream.WriteLine("    text-align: left;");
txtstream.WriteLine("    white-Space: nowrap;");
txtstream.WriteLine("}");
txtstream.WriteLine(".th");
txtstream.WriteLine("{");
txtstream.WriteLine("    BORDER-RIGHT: #999999 2px solid;");
txtstream.WriteLine("    PADDING-RIGHT: 6px;");
txtstream.WriteLine("    PADDING-LEFT: 6px;");
txtstream.WriteLine("    FONT-WEIGHT: Bold;");
txtstream.WriteLine("    PADDING-BOTTOM: 6px;");
txtstream.WriteLine("    COLOR: black;");
txtstream.WriteLine("    PADDING-TOP: 6px;");
txtstream.WriteLine("    BORDER-BOTTOM: #999 2px solid;");
txtstream.WriteLine("    BACKGROUND-COLOR: #eeeeee;");
txtstream.WriteLine("    FONT-FAMILY: font-family: Cambria, serif;");
txtstream.WriteLine("    FONT-SIZE: 10px;");
txtstream.WriteLine("    text-align: right;");
txtstream.WriteLine("    white-Space: nowrap;");
txtstream.WriteLine("}");
txtstream.WriteLine("td");
txtstream.WriteLine("{");
txtstream.WriteLine("    BORDER-RIGHT: #999999 3px solid;");
txtstream.WriteLine("    PADDING-RIGHT: 6px;");
txtstream.WriteLine("    PADDING-LEFT: 6px;");
txtstream.WriteLine("    FONT-WEIGHT: Normal;");
txtstream.WriteLine("    PADDING-BOTTOM: 6px;");
txtstream.WriteLine("    COLOR: navy;");
txtstream.WriteLine("    LINE-HEIGHT: 14px;");
txtstream.WriteLine("    PADDING-TOP: 6px;");
txtstream.WriteLine("    BORDER-BOTTOM: #999 1px solid;");
txtstream.WriteLine("    BACKGROUND-COLOR: #eeeeee;");
txtstream.WriteLine("    FONT-FAMILY: font-family: Cambria, serif;");
txtstream.WriteLine("    FONT-SIZE: 12px;");
txtstream.WriteLine("    text-align: left;");
txtstream.WriteLine("    white-Space: nowrap;");
txtstream.WriteLine("}");
txtstream.WriteLine("div");
txtstream.WriteLine("{");
txtstream.WriteLine("    BORDER-RIGHT: #999999 3px solid;");
```

```
txtstream.WriteLine("    PADDING-RIGHT: 6px;");
txtstream.WriteLine("    PADDING-LEFT: 6px;");
txtstream.WriteLine("    FONT-WEIGHT: Normal;");
txtstream.WriteLine("    PADDING-BOTTOM: 6px;");
txtstream.WriteLine("    COLOR: white;");
txtstream.WriteLine("    PADDING-TOP: 6px;");
txtstream.WriteLine("    BORDER-BOTTOM: #999 1px solid;");
txtstream.WriteLine("    BACKGROUND-COLOR: navy;");
txtstream.WriteLine("    FONT-FAMILY: font-family: Cambria, serif;");
txtstream.WriteLine("    FONT-SIZE: 10px;");
txtstream.WriteLine("    text-align: left;");
txtstream.WriteLine("    white-Space: nowrap;");
txtstream.WriteLine("}");
txtstream.WriteLine("span");
txtstream.WriteLine("{");
txtstream.WriteLine("    BORDER-RIGHT: #999999 3px solid;");
txtstream.WriteLine("    PADDING-RIGHT: 3px;");
txtstream.WriteLine("    PADDING-LEFT: 3px;");
txtstream.WriteLine("    FONT-WEIGHT: Normal;");
txtstream.WriteLine("    PADDING-BOTTOM: 3px;");
txtstream.WriteLine("    COLOR: white;");
txtstream.WriteLine("    PADDING-TOP: 3px;");
txtstream.WriteLine("    BORDER-BOTTOM: #999 1px solid;");
txtstream.WriteLine("    BACKGROUND-COLOR: navy;");
txtstream.WriteLine("    FONT-FAMILY: font-family: Cambria, serif;");
txtstream.WriteLine("    FONT-SIZE: 10px;");
txtstream.WriteLine("    text-align: left;");
txtstream.WriteLine("    white-Space: nowrap;");
txtstream.WriteLine("    display: inline-block;");
txtstream.WriteLine("    width: 100%;");
txtstream.WriteLine("}");
txtstream.WriteLine("textarea");
txtstream.WriteLine("{");
txtstream.WriteLine("    BORDER-RIGHT: #999999 3px solid;");
txtstream.WriteLine("    PADDING-RIGHT: 3px;");
txtstream.WriteLine("    PADDING-LEFT: 3px;");
txtstream.WriteLine("    FONT-WEIGHT: Normal;");
txtstream.WriteLine("    PADDING-BOTTOM: 3px;");
txtstream.WriteLine("    COLOR: white;");
txtstream.WriteLine("    PADDING-TOP: 3px;");
```

```
txtstream.WriteLine("    BORDER-BOTTOM: #999 1px solid;");
txtstream.WriteLine("    BACKGROUND-COLOR: navy;");
txtstream.WriteLine("    FONT-FAMILY: font-family: Cambria, serif;");
txtstream.WriteLine("    FONT-SIZE: 10px;");
txtstream.WriteLine("    text-align: left;");
txtstream.WriteLine("    white-Space: nowrap;");
txtstream.WriteLine("    width: 100%;");
txtstream.WriteLine("}");
txtstream.WriteLine("select");
txtstream.WriteLine("{");
txtstream.WriteLine("    BORDER-RIGHT: #999999 3px solid;");
txtstream.WriteLine("    PADDING-RIGHT: 6px;");
txtstream.WriteLine("    PADDING-LEFT: 6px;");
txtstream.WriteLine("    FONT-WEIGHT: Normal;");
txtstream.WriteLine("    PADDING-BOTTOM: 6px;");
txtstream.WriteLine("    COLOR: white;");
txtstream.WriteLine("    PADDING-TOP: 6px;");
txtstream.WriteLine("    BORDER-BOTTOM: #999 1px solid;");
txtstream.WriteLine("    BACKGROUND-COLOR: navy;");
txtstream.WriteLine("    FONT-FAMILY: font-family: Cambria, serif;");
txtstream.WriteLine("    FONT-SIZE: 10px;");
txtstream.WriteLine("    text-align: left;");
txtstream.WriteLine("    white-Space: nowrap;");
txtstream.WriteLine("    width: 100%;");
txtstream.WriteLine("}");
txtstream.WriteLine("input");
txtstream.WriteLine("{");
txtstream.WriteLine("    BORDER-RIGHT: #999999 3px solid;");
txtstream.WriteLine("    PADDING-RIGHT: 3px;");
txtstream.WriteLine("    PADDING-LEFT: 3px;");
txtstream.WriteLine("    FONT-WEIGHT: Bold;");
txtstream.WriteLine("    PADDING-BOTTOM: 3px;");
txtstream.WriteLine("    COLOR: white;");
txtstream.WriteLine("    PADDING-TOP: 3px;");
txtstream.WriteLine("    BORDER-BOTTOM: #999 1px solid;");
txtstream.WriteLine("    BACKGROUND-COLOR: navy;");
txtstream.WriteLine("    FONT-FAMILY: font-family: Cambria, serif;");
txtstream.WriteLine("    FONT-SIZE: 12px;");
txtstream.WriteLine("    text-align: left;");
txtstream.WriteLine("    display: table-cell;");
```

```
txtstream.WriteLine("    white-Space: nowrap;");
txtstream.WriteLine("    width: 100%;");
txtstream.WriteLine("}");
txtstream.WriteLine("h1 {");
txtstream.WriteLine("color: antiquewhite;");
txtstream.WriteLine("text-shadow: 1px 1px 1px black;");
txtstream.WriteLine("padding: 3px;");
txtstream.WriteLine("text-align: center;");
txtstream.WriteLine("box-shadow: inset 2px 2px 5px rgba(0,0,0,0.5), inset -2px -
2px 5px rgba(255,255,255,0.5)");
txtstream.WriteLine("}");
txtstream.WriteLine("</style>");
txtstream.WriteLine("</head>");
txtstream.WriteLine("<body>");
txtstream.WriteLine("<table Border='1' cellpadding='1' cellspacing='1'>");

switch (Orientation)
{
   case "Single-Line Horizontal":
   {
      for (var y = 0; y < Rows.Count; y++)
      {
         txtstream.WriteLine("<tr>");
         for (var x = 0; x < Names.Count; x++)
         {
            txtstream.WriteLine("<th>" + Names(x) + "</th>");
         }
         txtstream.WriteLine("</tr>");
         txtstream.WriteLine("<tr>");
         for (var x = 0; x < Names.Count; x++)
         {
            var value = Rows(y)(x);
            txtstream.WriteLine("<td>" + value + "</td>");
         }
         txtstream.WriteLine("</tr>");
         break;
      }
      break;
   }
   case "Multi-Line Horizontal":
```

```
{
   txtstream.WriteLine("<tr>");
   for (var x = 0; x < Names.Count; x++)
   {
       txtstream.WriteLine("<th>" + Names(x) + "</th>");
   }
   txtstream.WriteLine("</tr>");
   for (var y = 0; y < Rows.Count; y++)
   {
     txtstream.WriteLine("<tr>");
     for (var x = 0; x < Names.Count; x++)
     {
       var value = Rows(y)(x);
       txtstream.WriteLine("<td>" + value + "</td>");
     }
     txtstream.WriteLine("</tr>");
   }
   break;
}
case "Single-Line Vertical":
{
   for (var y = 0; y < Rows.Count; y++)
   {
     for (var x = 0; x < Names.Count; x++)
     {
       txtstream.WriteLine("<tr><th>" + Names(x) + "</th><td>" + Rows(y)(x) +
"</td></tr>");
     }
     break;
   }
   break;
}
case "Multi-Line Vertical":
{
   for (var x = 0; x < Names.Count; x++)
   {
     txtstream.WriteLine("<tr><th>" + Names(x) + "</th>");
     for (var y = 0; y < Rows.Count; y++)
     {
       var value = Rows(y)(x);
```

```
        txtstream.WriteLine("<td>" + value + "</td>");
      }
      txtstream.WriteLine("</tr>");
    }
    break;
  }
}
txtstream.WriteLine("</table>");
txtstream.WriteLine("</body>");
txtstream.WriteLine("</html>");
txtstream.Close();

function GetValue(Name, obj)
{
   var tempstr = new String();
   var tempstr1 = new String();
   var tName = new String();
   tempstr1 = obj.GetObjectText_();
   var re = /"/g;
   tempstr1 = tempstr1.replace(re , "");
   var pos;
   tName = Name + " = ";
   pos = tempstr1.indexOf(tName);
   if (pos > -1)
   {
     pos = pos + tName.length;
     tempstr = tempstr1.substring(pos, tempstr1.length);
     pos = tempstr.indexOf(";");
     tempstr = tempstr.substring(0, pos);
     tempstr = tempstr.replace("{", "");
     tempstr = tempstr.replace("}", "");
     if (tempstr.length > 13)
     {
        if (obj.Properties_(Name).CIMType == 101)
        {
          tempstr = tempstr.substr(4, 2) + "/"  + tempstr.substr(6, 2) + "/" +
tempstr.substr(0, 3) + " " + tempstr.substr(8, 2) + ":" + tempstr.substr(10, 2) + ":" +
tempstr.substr(12, 2);
        }
     }
```

```
    return tempstr;
    }
    else
    {
    return "";
    }
}
```

CREATE ASP CODE

Inside this sub routine is the code to create an ASP Webpage.

```
var ws = new ActiveXObject("WScript.Shell");
var fso = new ActiveXObject("Scripting.FileSystemObject");
txtstream = fso.OpenTextFile(ws.CurrentDirectory + "\\Process.asp", 2,
true, -2);

txtstream.WriteLine("<html
xmlns=\"http://www.w3.org/1999/xhtml\">");
txtstream.WriteLine("<head>");
txtstream.WriteLine("<title>Win32_Process</title>");
txtstream.WriteLine("<style type='text/css'>");
txtstream.WriteLine("body");
txtstream.WriteLine("{");
txtstream.WriteLine("   PADDING-RIGHT: 0px;");
txtstream.WriteLine("   PADDING-LEFT: 0px;");
txtstream.WriteLine("   PADDING-BOTTOM: 0px;");
txtstream.WriteLine("   MARGIN: 0px;");
txtstream.WriteLine("   COLOR: #333;");
txtstream.WriteLine("   PADDING-TOP: 0px;");
txtstream.WriteLine("    FONT-FAMILY: verdana, arial, helvetica, sans-
serif;");
txtstream.WriteLine("}");
txtstream.WriteLine("table");
```

```
txtstream.WriteLine("{");
txtstream.WriteLine("    BORDER-RIGHT: #999999 1px solid;");
txtstream.WriteLine("    PADDING-RIGHT: 1px;");
txtstream.WriteLine("    PADDING-LEFT: 1px;");
txtstream.WriteLine("    PADDING-BOTTOM: 1px;");
txtstream.WriteLine("    LINE-HEIGHT: 8px;");
txtstream.WriteLine("    PADDING-TOP: 1px;");
txtstream.WriteLine("    BORDER-BOTTOM: #999 1px solid;");
txtstream.WriteLine("    BACKGROUND-COLOR: #eeeeee;");
txtstream.WriteLine("
filter:progid:DXImageTransform.Microsoft.Shadow(color='silver',    Direction=135,
Strength=16)");
txtstream.WriteLine("}");
txtstream.WriteLine("th");
txtstream.WriteLine("{");
txtstream.WriteLine("    BORDER-RIGHT: #999999 3px solid;");
txtstream.WriteLine("    PADDING-RIGHT: 6px;");
txtstream.WriteLine("    PADDING-LEFT: 6px;");
txtstream.WriteLine("    FONT-WEIGHT: Bold;");
txtstream.WriteLine("    FONT-SIZE: 14px;");
txtstream.WriteLine("    PADDING-BOTTOM: 6px;");
txtstream.WriteLine("    COLOR: darkred;");
txtstream.WriteLine("    LINE-HEIGHT: 14px;");
txtstream.WriteLine("    PADDING-TOP: 6px;");
txtstream.WriteLine("    BORDER-BOTTOM: #999 1px solid;");
txtstream.WriteLine("    BACKGROUND-COLOR: #eeeeee;");
txtstream.WriteLine("    FONT-FAMILY: font-family: Cambria, serif;");
txtstream.WriteLine("    FONT-SIZE: 12px;");
txtstream.WriteLine("    text-align: left;");
txtstream.WriteLine("    white-Space: nowrap;");
txtstream.WriteLine("}");
txtstream.WriteLine(".th");
txtstream.WriteLine("{");
```

```
txtstream.WriteLine("    BORDER-RIGHT: #999999 2px solid;");
txtstream.WriteLine("    PADDING-RIGHT: 6px;");
txtstream.WriteLine("    PADDING-LEFT: 6px;");
txtstream.WriteLine("    FONT-WEIGHT: Bold;");
txtstream.WriteLine("    PADDING-BOTTOM: 6px;");
txtstream.WriteLine("    COLOR: black;");
txtstream.WriteLine("    PADDING-TOP: 6px;");
txtstream.WriteLine("    BORDER-BOTTOM: #999 2px solid;");
txtstream.WriteLine("    BACKGROUND-COLOR: #eeeeee;");
txtstream.WriteLine("    FONT-FAMILY: font-family: Cambria, serif;");
txtstream.WriteLine("    FONT-SIZE: 10px;");
txtstream.WriteLine("    text-align: right;");
txtstream.WriteLine("    white-Space: nowrap;");
txtstream.WriteLine("}");
txtstream.WriteLine("td");
txtstream.WriteLine("{");
txtstream.WriteLine("    BORDER-RIGHT: #999999 3px solid;");
txtstream.WriteLine("    PADDING-RIGHT: 6px;");
txtstream.WriteLine("    PADDING-LEFT: 6px;");
txtstream.WriteLine("    FONT-WEIGHT: Normal;");
txtstream.WriteLine("    PADDING-BOTTOM: 6px;");
txtstream.WriteLine("    COLOR: navy;");
txtstream.WriteLine("    LINE-HEIGHT: 14px;");
txtstream.WriteLine("    PADDING-TOP: 6px;");
txtstream.WriteLine("    BORDER-BOTTOM: #999 1px solid;");
txtstream.WriteLine("    BACKGROUND-COLOR: #eeeeee;");
txtstream.WriteLine("    FONT-FAMILY: font-family: Cambria, serif;");
txtstream.WriteLine("    FONT-SIZE: 12px;");
txtstream.WriteLine("    text-align: left;");
txtstream.WriteLine("    white-Space: nowrap;");
txtstream.WriteLine("}");
txtstream.WriteLine("div");
txtstream.WriteLine("{");
```

```
txtstream.WriteLine("    BORDER-RIGHT: #999999 3px solid;");
txtstream.WriteLine("    PADDING-RIGHT: 6px;");
txtstream.WriteLine("    PADDING-LEFT: 6px;");
txtstream.WriteLine("    FONT-WEIGHT: Normal;");
txtstream.WriteLine("    PADDING-BOTTOM: 6px;");
txtstream.WriteLine("    COLOR: white;");
txtstream.WriteLine("    PADDING-TOP: 6px;");
txtstream.WriteLine("    BORDER-BOTTOM: #999 1px solid;");
txtstream.WriteLine("    BACKGROUND-COLOR: navy;");
txtstream.WriteLine("    FONT-FAMILY: font-family: Cambria, serif;");
txtstream.WriteLine("    FONT-SIZE: 10px;");
txtstream.WriteLine("    text-align: left;");
txtstream.WriteLine("    white-Space: nowrap;");
txtstream.WriteLine("}");
txtstream.WriteLine("span");
txtstream.WriteLine("{");
txtstream.WriteLine("    BORDER-RIGHT: #999999 3px solid;");
txtstream.WriteLine("    PADDING-RIGHT: 3px;");
txtstream.WriteLine("    PADDING-LEFT: 3px;");
txtstream.WriteLine("    FONT-WEIGHT: Normal;");
txtstream.WriteLine("    PADDING-BOTTOM: 3px;");
txtstream.WriteLine("    COLOR: white;");
txtstream.WriteLine("    PADDING-TOP: 3px;");
txtstream.WriteLine("    BORDER-BOTTOM: #999 1px solid;");
txtstream.WriteLine("    BACKGROUND-COLOR: navy;");
txtstream.WriteLine("    FONT-FAMILY: font-family: Cambria, serif;");
txtstream.WriteLine("    FONT-SIZE: 10px;");
txtstream.WriteLine("    text-align: left;");
txtstream.WriteLine("    white-Space: nowrap;");
txtstream.WriteLine("    display: inline-block;");
txtstream.WriteLine("    width: 100%;");
txtstream.WriteLine("}");
txtstream.WriteLine("textarea");
```

```
txtstream.WriteLine("{“);
txtstream.WriteLine("    BORDER-RIGHT: #999999 3px solid;”);
txtstream.WriteLine("    PADDING-RIGHT: 3px;”);
txtstream.WriteLine("    PADDING-LEFT: 3px;”);
txtstream.WriteLine("    FONT-WEIGHT: Normal;”);
txtstream.WriteLine("    PADDING-BOTTOM: 3px;”);
txtstream.WriteLine("    COLOR: white;”);
txtstream.WriteLine("    PADDING-TOP: 3px;”);
txtstream.WriteLine("    BORDER-BOTTOM: #999 1px solid;”);
txtstream.WriteLine("    BACKGROUND-COLOR: navy;”);
txtstream.WriteLine("    FONT-FAMILY: font-family: Cambria, serif;”);
txtstream.WriteLine("    FONT-SIZE: 10px;”);
txtstream.WriteLine("    text-align: left;”);
txtstream.WriteLine("    white-Space: nowrap;”);
txtstream.WriteLine("    width: 100%;”);
txtstream.WriteLine("}”);
txtstream.WriteLine("select”);
txtstream.WriteLine("{“);
txtstream.WriteLine("    BORDER-RIGHT: #999999 3px solid;”);
txtstream.WriteLine("    PADDING-RIGHT: 6px;”);
txtstream.WriteLine("    PADDING-LEFT: 6px;”);
txtstream.WriteLine("    FONT-WEIGHT: Normal;”);
txtstream.WriteLine("    PADDING-BOTTOM: 6px;”);
txtstream.WriteLine("    COLOR: white;”);
txtstream.WriteLine("    PADDING-TOP: 6px;”);
txtstream.WriteLine("    BORDER-BOTTOM: #999 1px solid;”);
txtstream.WriteLine("    BACKGROUND-COLOR: navy;”);
txtstream.WriteLine("    FONT-FAMILY: font-family: Cambria, serif;”);
txtstream.WriteLine("    FONT-SIZE: 10px;”);
txtstream.WriteLine("    text-align: left;”);
txtstream.WriteLine("    white-Space: nowrap;”);
txtstream.WriteLine("    width: 100%;”);
txtstream.WriteLine("}”);
```

```
txtstream.WriteLine("input");
txtstream.WriteLine("{");
txtstream.WriteLine("    BORDER-RIGHT: #999999 3px solid;");
txtstream.WriteLine("    PADDING-RIGHT: 3px;");
txtstream.WriteLine("    PADDING-LEFT: 3px;");
txtstream.WriteLine("    FONT-WEIGHT: Bold;");
txtstream.WriteLine("    PADDING-BOTTOM: 3px;");
txtstream.WriteLine("    COLOR: white;");
txtstream.WriteLine("    PADDING-TOP: 3px;");
txtstream.WriteLine("    BORDER-BOTTOM: #999 1px solid;");
txtstream.WriteLine("    BACKGROUND-COLOR: navy;");
txtstream.WriteLine("    FONT-FAMILY: font-family: Cambria, serif;");
txtstream.WriteLine("    FONT-SIZE: 12px;");
txtstream.WriteLine("    text-align: left;");
txtstream.WriteLine("    display: table-cell;");
txtstream.WriteLine("    white-Space: nowrap;");
txtstream.WriteLine("    width: 100%;");
txtstream.WriteLine("}");
txtstream.WriteLine("h1 {");
txtstream.WriteLine("color: antiquewhite;");
txtstream.WriteLine("text-shadow: 1px 1px 1px black;");
txtstream.WriteLine("padding: 3px;");
txtstream.WriteLine("text-align: center;");
txtstream.WriteLine("box-shadow: inset 2px 2px 5px rgba(0,0,0,0.5),
inset -2px -2px 5px rgba(255,255,255,0.5)");
txtstream.WriteLine("}");
txtstream.WriteLine("</style>");
txtstream.WriteLine("</head>");
txtstream.WriteLine("<body>");
txtstream.WriteLine("<%");
txtstream.WriteLine("Response.Write(\"<table           Border='1'
cellpadding='1' cellspacing='1'>\" + vbcrlf)");
```

```
switch (Orientation)
{
    case "Single-Line Horizontal":
        {
            for (var y = 0; y < Rows.Count; y++)
            {
                txtstream.WriteLine("Response.Write(\"<tr>\" + vbcrlf)");
                for (var x = 0; x < Names.Count; x++)
                {
                    txtstream.WriteLine("Response.Write(\"<th>" + Names(x)
+ "</th>\" + vbcrlf)");
                }
                txtstream.WriteLine("Response.Write(\"</tr>\" + vbcrlf)");
                txtstream.WriteLine("Response.Write(\"<tr>\" + vbcrlf)");
                for (var x = 0; x < Names.Count; x++)
                {
                    String value = Rows(y)(x);
                    txtstream.WriteLine("Response.Write(\"<td>" + value +
"</td>\" + vbcrlf)");
                }
                txtstream.WriteLine("Response.Write(\"</tr>\" + vbcrlf)");
                break;
            }
            break;
        }

    case "Multi-Line Horizontal":
        {

            for (var y = 0; y < Rows.Count; y++)
            {
                txtstream.WriteLine("Response.Write(\"<tr>\" + vbcrlf)");
```

```
                    for (var x = 0; x < Names.Count; x++)
                    {
                        txtstream.WriteLine("Response.Write(\"<th>"   +   Names(x)
+ "</th>\" + vbcrlf)");
                    }
                    txtstream.WriteLine("Response.Write(\"</tr>\" + vbcrlf)");
                    break;
                }
                for (var y = 0; y < Rows.Count; y++)
                {
                    txtstream.WriteLine("Response.Write(\"<tr>\" + vbcrlf)");
                    for (var x = 0; x < Names.Count; x++)
                    {
                        string value = Rows(y)(x);
                        txtstream.WriteLine("Response.Write(\"<td>"   +   value   +
"</td>\" + vbcrlf)");
                    }
                    txtstream.WriteLine("Response.Write(\"</tr>\" + vbcrlf)");
                }
                break;
            }
        case "Single-Line Vertical":
            {

                for (var y = 0; y < Rows.Count; y++)
                {

                    for (var x = 0; x < Names.Count; x++)
                    {
                        txtstream.WriteLine("Response.Write(\"<tr><th>"              +
Names(x) + "</th><td>" + Rows(y)(x) + "</td></tr>\" + vbcrlf)");
                    }
                    break;
```

```
                    }
                 break;
              }

           case "Multi-Line Vertical":
              {

                 for (var x = 0; x < Names.Count; x++)
                 {

                    txtstream.WriteLine("Response.Write(\"<tr><th>"              +
Names(x) + "</th>\" + vbcrlf)");
                       for (var y = 0; y < Rows.Count; y++)
                       {
                          string value = Rows(y)(x);
                          txtstream.WriteLine("Response.Write(\"<td>"   +   value   +
"</td>\" + vbcrlf)");
                       }
                       txtstream.WriteLine("Response.Write(\"</tr>\" + vbcrlf)");
                 }
                 break;
              }

        }
        txtstream.WriteLine("Response.Write(\"</table>\" + vbcrlf)");
        txtstream.WriteLine("%>");
        txtstream.WriteLine("</body>");
        txtstream.WriteLine("</html>");
        txtstream.Close();
     }
```

CREATE ASPX CODE

Inside this sub routine is the code to create an ASPX Webpage.

```
var ws = new ActiveXObject("WScript.Shell");
var fso = new ActiveXObject("Scripting.FileSystemObject");
txtstream = fso.OpenTextFile(ws.CurrentDirectory + "\\Process.asp", 2, true, -2);

txtstream.WriteLine("<!DOCTYPE html PUBLIC \"-//W3C//DTD XHTML 1.0 Transitional//EN\" \"http://www.w3.org/TR/xhtml1/DTD/xhtml1-transitional.dtd\">");
txtstream.WriteLine("");
txtstream.WriteLine("<html xmlns=\"http://www.w3.org/1999/xhtml\">");
txtstream.WriteLine("<head>");
txtstream.WriteLine("<title>Win32_Process</title>");
txtstream.WriteLine("<style type='text/css'>");
txtstream.WriteLine("body");
txtstream.WriteLine("{");
txtstream.WriteLine("    PADDING-RIGHT: 0px;");
txtstream.WriteLine("    PADDING-LEFT: 0px;");
txtstream.WriteLine("    PADDING-BOTTOM: 0px;");
txtstream.WriteLine("    MARGIN: 0px;");
txtstream.WriteLine("    COLOR: #333;");
txtstream.WriteLine("    PADDING-TOP: 0px;");
txtstream.WriteLine("    FONT-FAMILY: verdana, arial, helvetica, sans-serif;");
```

```
txtstream.WriteLine("}");
txtstream.WriteLine("table");
txtstream.WriteLine("{");
txtstream.WriteLine("   BORDER-RIGHT: #999999 1px solid;");
txtstream.WriteLine("   PADDING-RIGHT: 1px;");
txtstream.WriteLine("   PADDING-LEFT: 1px;");
txtstream.WriteLine("   PADDING-BOTTOM: 1px;");
txtstream.WriteLine("   LINE-HEIGHT: 8px;");
txtstream.WriteLine("   PADDING-TOP: 1px;");
txtstream.WriteLine("   BORDER-BOTTOM: #999 1px solid;");
txtstream.WriteLine("   BACKGROUND-COLOR: #eeeeee;");
txtstream.WriteLine("
filter:progid:DXImageTransform.Microsoft.Shadow(color='silver',     Direction=135,
Strength=16)");
txtstream.WriteLine("}");
txtstream.WriteLine("th");
txtstream.WriteLine("{");
txtstream.WriteLine("   BORDER-RIGHT: #999999 3px solid;");
txtstream.WriteLine("   PADDING-RIGHT: 6px;");
txtstream.WriteLine("   PADDING-LEFT: 6px;");
txtstream.WriteLine("   FONT-WEIGHT: Bold;");
txtstream.WriteLine("   FONT-SIZE: 14px;");
txtstream.WriteLine("   PADDING-BOTTOM: 6px;");
txtstream.WriteLine("   COLOR: darkred;");
txtstream.WriteLine("   LINE-HEIGHT: 14px;");
txtstream.WriteLine("   PADDING-TOP: 6px;");
txtstream.WriteLine("   BORDER-BOTTOM: #999 1px solid;");
txtstream.WriteLine("   BACKGROUND-COLOR: #eeeeee;");
txtstream.WriteLine("   FONT-FAMILY: font-family: Cambria, serif;");
txtstream.WriteLine("   FONT-SIZE: 12px;");
txtstream.WriteLine("   text-align: left;");
txtstream.WriteLine("   white-Space: nowrap;");
txtstream.WriteLine("}");
```

```
txtstream.WriteLine(".th");
txtstream.WriteLine("{");
txtstream.WriteLine("    BORDER-RIGHT: #999999 2px solid;");
txtstream.WriteLine("    PADDING-RIGHT: 6px;");
txtstream.WriteLine("    PADDING-LEFT: 6px;");
txtstream.WriteLine("    FONT-WEIGHT: Bold;");
txtstream.WriteLine("    PADDING-BOTTOM: 6px;");
txtstream.WriteLine("    COLOR: black;");
txtstream.WriteLine("    PADDING-TOP: 6px;");
txtstream.WriteLine("    BORDER-BOTTOM: #999 2px solid;");
txtstream.WriteLine("    BACKGROUND-COLOR: #eeeeee;");
txtstream.WriteLine("    FONT-FAMILY: font-family: Cambria, serif;");
txtstream.WriteLine("    FONT-SIZE: 10px;");
txtstream.WriteLine("    text-align: right;");
txtstream.WriteLine("    white-Space: nowrap;");
txtstream.WriteLine("}");
txtstream.WriteLine("td");
txtstream.WriteLine("{");
txtstream.WriteLine("    BORDER-RIGHT: #999999 3px solid;");
txtstream.WriteLine("    PADDING-RIGHT: 6px;");
txtstream.WriteLine("    PADDING-LEFT: 6px;");
txtstream.WriteLine("    FONT-WEIGHT: Normal;");
txtstream.WriteLine("    PADDING-BOTTOM: 6px;");
txtstream.WriteLine("    COLOR: navy;");
txtstream.WriteLine("    LINE-HEIGHT: 14px;");
txtstream.WriteLine("    PADDING-TOP: 6px;");
txtstream.WriteLine("    BORDER-BOTTOM: #999 1px solid;");
txtstream.WriteLine("    BACKGROUND-COLOR: #eeeeee;");
txtstream.WriteLine("    FONT-FAMILY: font-family: Cambria, serif;");
txtstream.WriteLine("    FONT-SIZE: 12px;");
txtstream.WriteLine("    text-align: left;");
txtstream.WriteLine("    white-Space: nowrap;");
txtstream.WriteLine("}");
```

```
txtstream.WriteLine("div");
txtstream.WriteLine("{");
txtstream.WriteLine("    BORDER-RIGHT: #999999 3px solid;");
txtstream.WriteLine("    PADDING-RIGHT: 6px;");
txtstream.WriteLine("    PADDING-LEFT: 6px;");
txtstream.WriteLine("    FONT-WEIGHT: Normal;");
txtstream.WriteLine("    PADDING-BOTTOM: 6px;");
txtstream.WriteLine("    COLOR: white;");
txtstream.WriteLine("    PADDING-TOP: 6px;");
txtstream.WriteLine("    BORDER-BOTTOM: #999 1px solid;");
txtstream.WriteLine("    BACKGROUND-COLOR: navy;");
txtstream.WriteLine("    FONT-FAMILY: font-family: Cambria, serif;");
txtstream.WriteLine("    FONT-SIZE: 10px;");
txtstream.WriteLine("    text-align: left;");
txtstream.WriteLine("    white-Space: nowrap;");
txtstream.WriteLine("}");
txtstream.WriteLine("span");
txtstream.WriteLine("{");
txtstream.WriteLine("    BORDER-RIGHT: #999999 3px solid;");
txtstream.WriteLine("    PADDING-RIGHT: 3px;");
txtstream.WriteLine("    PADDING-LEFT: 3px;");
txtstream.WriteLine("    FONT-WEIGHT: Normal;");
txtstream.WriteLine("    PADDING-BOTTOM: 3px;");
txtstream.WriteLine("    COLOR: white;");
txtstream.WriteLine("    PADDING-TOP: 3px;");
txtstream.WriteLine("    BORDER-BOTTOM: #999 1px solid;");
txtstream.WriteLine("    BACKGROUND-COLOR: navy;");
txtstream.WriteLine("    FONT-FAMILY: font-family: Cambria, serif;");
txtstream.WriteLine("    FONT-SIZE: 10px;");
txtstream.WriteLine("    text-align: left;");
txtstream.WriteLine("    white-Space: nowrap;");
txtstream.WriteLine("    display: inline-block;");
txtstream.WriteLine("    width: 100%;");
```

```
txtstream.WriteLine("}");
txtstream.WriteLine("textarea");
txtstream.WriteLine("{");
txtstream.WriteLine("    BORDER-RIGHT: #999999 3px solid;");
txtstream.WriteLine("    PADDING-RIGHT: 3px;");
txtstream.WriteLine("    PADDING-LEFT: 3px;");
txtstream.WriteLine("    FONT-WEIGHT: Normal;");
txtstream.WriteLine("    PADDING-BOTTOM: 3px;");
txtstream.WriteLine("    COLOR: white;");
txtstream.WriteLine("    PADDING-TOP: 3px;");
txtstream.WriteLine("    BORDER-BOTTOM: #999 1px solid;");
txtstream.WriteLine("    BACKGROUND-COLOR: navy;");
txtstream.WriteLine("    FONT-FAMILY: font-family: Cambria, serif;");
txtstream.WriteLine("    FONT-SIZE: 10px;");
txtstream.WriteLine("    text-align: left;");
txtstream.WriteLine("    white-Space: nowrap;");
txtstream.WriteLine("    width: 100%;");
txtstream.WriteLine("}");
txtstream.WriteLine("select");
txtstream.WriteLine("{");
txtstream.WriteLine("    BORDER-RIGHT: #999999 3px solid;");
txtstream.WriteLine("    PADDING-RIGHT: 6px;");
txtstream.WriteLine("    PADDING-LEFT: 6px;");
txtstream.WriteLine("    FONT-WEIGHT: Normal;");
txtstream.WriteLine("    PADDING-BOTTOM: 6px;");
txtstream.WriteLine("    COLOR: white;");
txtstream.WriteLine("    PADDING-TOP: 6px;");
txtstream.WriteLine("    BORDER-BOTTOM: #999 1px solid;");
txtstream.WriteLine("    BACKGROUND-COLOR: navy;");
txtstream.WriteLine("    FONT-FAMILY: font-family: Cambria, serif;");
txtstream.WriteLine("    FONT-SIZE: 10px;");
txtstream.WriteLine("    text-align: left;");
txtstream.WriteLine("    white-Space: nowrap;");
```

```
txtstream.WriteLine("    width: 100%;");
txtstream.WriteLine("}");
txtstream.WriteLine("input");
txtstream.WriteLine("{");
txtstream.WriteLine("    BORDER-RIGHT: #999999 3px solid;");
txtstream.WriteLine("    PADDING-RIGHT: 3px;");
txtstream.WriteLine("    PADDING-LEFT: 3px;");
txtstream.WriteLine("    FONT-WEIGHT: Bold;");
txtstream.WriteLine("    PADDING-BOTTOM: 3px;");
txtstream.WriteLine("    COLOR: white;");
txtstream.WriteLine("    PADDING-TOP: 3px;");
txtstream.WriteLine("    BORDER-BOTTOM: #999 1px solid;");
txtstream.WriteLine("    BACKGROUND-COLOR: navy;");
txtstream.WriteLine("    FONT-FAMILY: font-family: Cambria, serif;");
txtstream.WriteLine("    FONT-SIZE: 12px;");
txtstream.WriteLine("    text-align: left;");
txtstream.WriteLine("    display: table-cell;");
txtstream.WriteLine("    white-Space: nowrap;");
txtstream.WriteLine("    width: 100%;");
txtstream.WriteLine("}");
txtstream.WriteLine("h1 {");
txtstream.WriteLine("color: antiquewhite;");
txtstream.WriteLine("text-shadow: 1px 1px 1px black;");
txtstream.WriteLine("padding: 3px;");
txtstream.WriteLine("text-align: center;");
txtstream.WriteLine("box-shadow: inset 2px 2px 5px rgba(0,0,0,0.5),
inset -2px -2px 5px rgba(255,255,255,0.5)");
txtstream.WriteLine("}");
txtstream.WriteLine("</style>");
txtstream.WriteLine("</head>");
txtstream.WriteLine("<body>");
txtstream.WriteLine("<%");
```

```
txtstream.WriteLine("Response.Write(\"<table                    Border='1'
cellpadding='1' cellspacing='1'>\" + vbcrlf)");


        switch (Orientation)
        {


            case "Single-Line Horizontal":
                {
                    for (var y = 0; y < Rows.Count; y++)
                    {
                        txtstream.WriteLine("Response.Write(\"<tr>\" + vbcrlf)");
                        for (var x = 0; x < Names.Count; x++)
                        {
                            txtstream.WriteLine("Response.Write(\"<th>"  +  Names(x)
+ "</th>\" + vbcrlf)");
                        }
                        txtstream.WriteLine("Response.Write(\"</tr>\" + vbcrlf)");
                        txtstream.WriteLine("Response.Write(\"<tr>\" + vbcrlf)");
                        for (var x = 0; x < Names.Count; x++)
                        {
                            String value = Rows(y)(x);
                            txtstream.WriteLine("Response.Write(\"<td>"  +  value  +
"</td>\" + vbcrlf)");
                        }
                        txtstream.WriteLine("Response.Write(\"</tr>\" + vbcrlf)");
                        break;
                    }
                    break;
                }

            case "Multi-Line Horizontal":
```

```
                {

                    for (var y = 0; y < Rows.Count; y++)
                    {
                       txtstream.WriteLine("Response.Write(\"<tr>\" + vbcrlf)");
                       for (var x = 0; x < Names.Count; x++)
                       {
                          txtstream.WriteLine("Response.Write(\"<th>" + Names(x)
+ "</th>\" + vbcrlf)");
                       }
                       txtstream.WriteLine("Response.Write(\"</tr>\" + vbcrlf)");
                       break;
                    }
                    for (var y = 0; y < Rows.Count; y++)
                    {
                       txtstream.WriteLine("Response.Write(\"<tr>\" + vbcrlf)");
                       for (var x = 0; x < Names.Count; x++)
                       {
                          string value = Rows(y)(x);
                          txtstream.WriteLine("Response.Write(\"<td>" + value +
"</td>\" + vbcrlf)");
                       }
                       txtstream.WriteLine("Response.Write(\"</tr>\" + vbcrlf)");
                    }
                    break;
                }
            case "Single-Line Vertical":
                {

                    for (var y = 0; y < Rows.Count; y++)
                    {

                       for (var x = 0; x < Names.Count; x++)
```

```
                {
                    txtstream.WriteLine("Response.Write(\"<tr><th>"              +
Names(x) + "</th><td>" + Rows(y)(x) + "</td></tr>\" + vbcrlf)");
                }
                break;
            }
            break;
        }

        case "Multi-Line Vertical":
        {

            for (var x = 0; x < Names.Count; x++)
            {

                txtstream.WriteLine("Response.Write(\"<tr><th>"              +
Names(x) + "</th>\" + vbcrlf)");
                for (var y = 0; y < Rows.Count; y++)
                {
                    string value = Rows(y)(x);
                    txtstream.WriteLine("Response.Write(\"<td>"   +   value   +
"</td>\" + vbcrlf)");
                }
                txtstream.WriteLine("Response.Write(\"</tr>\" + vbcrlf)");
            }
            break;
        }

    }
    txtstream.WriteLine("Response.Write(\"</table>\" + vbcrlf)");
    txtstream.WriteLine("%>");
    txtstream.WriteLine("</body>");
    txtstream.WriteLine("</html>");
```

```
txtstream.Close();
txtstream.WriteLine("</body>");
txtstream.WriteLine("</html>");
txtstream.Close();
```

CREATE HTA CODE

Inside this sub routine is the code to create an HTA Application.

```
var ws = new ActiveXObject("WScript.Shell");
var fso = new ActiveXObject("Scripting.FileSystemObject");
txtstream = fso.OpenTextFile(ws.CurrentDirectory + "\\Process.hta", 2,
true, -2);

txtstream.WriteLine("<html>");
txtstream.WriteLine("<head>");
txtstream.WriteLine("<HTA:APPLICATION ");
txtstream.WriteLine("ID = \"Process\" ");
txtstream.WriteLine("APPLICATIONNAME = \"Process\" ");
txtstream.WriteLine("SCROLL = \"yes\" ");
txtstream.WriteLine("SINGLEINSTANCE = \"yes\" ");
txtstream.WriteLine("WINDOWSTATE = \"maximize\" >");
txtstream.WriteLine("<title>Win32_Process</title>");
txtstream.WriteLine("<style type='text/css'>");
txtstream.WriteLine("body");
txtstream.WriteLine("{");
txtstream.WriteLine("   PADDING-RIGHT: 0px;");
txtstream.WriteLine("   PADDING-LEFT: 0px;");
txtstream.WriteLine("   PADDING-BOTTOM: 0px;");
txtstream.WriteLine("   MARGIN: 0px;");
txtstream.WriteLine("   COLOR: #333;");
txtstream.WriteLine("   PADDING-TOP: 0px;");
txtstream.WriteLine("    FONT-FAMILY: verdana, arial, helvetica, sans-
serif;");
```

```
txtstream.WriteLine("}");
txtstream.WriteLine("table");
txtstream.WriteLine("{");
txtstream.WriteLine("    BORDER-RIGHT: #999999 1px solid;");
txtstream.WriteLine("    PADDING-RIGHT: 1px;");
txtstream.WriteLine("    PADDING-LEFT: 1px;");
txtstream.WriteLine("    PADDING-BOTTOM: 1px;");
txtstream.WriteLine("    LINE-HEIGHT: 8px;");
txtstream.WriteLine("    PADDING-TOP: 1px;");
txtstream.WriteLine("    BORDER-BOTTOM: #999 1px solid;");
txtstream.WriteLine("    BACKGROUND-COLOR: #eeeeee;");
txtstream.WriteLine("
filter:progid:DXImageTransform.Microsoft.Shadow(color='silver',       Direction=135,
Strength=16)");
txtstream.WriteLine("}");
txtstream.WriteLine("th");
txtstream.WriteLine("{");
txtstream.WriteLine("    BORDER-RIGHT: #999999 3px solid;");
txtstream.WriteLine("    PADDING-RIGHT: 6px;");
txtstream.WriteLine("    PADDING-LEFT: 6px;");
txtstream.WriteLine("    FONT-WEIGHT: Bold;");
txtstream.WriteLine("    FONT-SIZE: 14px;");
txtstream.WriteLine("    PADDING-BOTTOM: 6px;");
txtstream.WriteLine("    COLOR: darkred;");
txtstream.WriteLine("    LINE-HEIGHT: 14px;");
txtstream.WriteLine("    PADDING-TOP: 6px;");
txtstream.WriteLine("    BORDER-BOTTOM: #999 1px solid;");
txtstream.WriteLine("    BACKGROUND-COLOR: #eeeeee;");
txtstream.WriteLine("    FONT-FAMILY: font-family: Cambria, serif;");
txtstream.WriteLine("    FONT-SIZE: 12px;");
txtstream.WriteLine("    text-align: left;");
txtstream.WriteLine("    white-Space: nowrap;");
txtstream.WriteLine("}");
```

```
txtstream.WriteLine(".th");
txtstream.WriteLine("{");
txtstream.WriteLine("    BORDER-RIGHT: #999999 2px solid;");
txtstream.WriteLine("    PADDING-RIGHT: 6px;");
txtstream.WriteLine("    PADDING-LEFT: 6px;");
txtstream.WriteLine("    FONT-WEIGHT: Bold;");
txtstream.WriteLine("    PADDING-BOTTOM: 6px;");
txtstream.WriteLine("    COLOR: black;");
txtstream.WriteLine("    PADDING-TOP: 6px;");
txtstream.WriteLine("    BORDER-BOTTOM: #999 2px solid;");
txtstream.WriteLine("    BACKGROUND-COLOR: #eeeeee;");
txtstream.WriteLine("    FONT-FAMILY: font-family: Cambria, serif;");
txtstream.WriteLine("    FONT-SIZE: 10px;");
txtstream.WriteLine("    text-align: right;");
txtstream.WriteLine("    white-Space: nowrap;");
txtstream.WriteLine("}");
txtstream.WriteLine("td");
txtstream.WriteLine("{");
txtstream.WriteLine("    BORDER-RIGHT: #999999 3px solid;");
txtstream.WriteLine("    PADDING-RIGHT: 6px;");
txtstream.WriteLine("    PADDING-LEFT: 6px;");
txtstream.WriteLine("    FONT-WEIGHT: Normal;");
txtstream.WriteLine("    PADDING-BOTTOM: 6px;");
txtstream.WriteLine("    COLOR: navy;");
txtstream.WriteLine("    LINE-HEIGHT: 14px;");
txtstream.WriteLine("    PADDING-TOP: 6px;");
txtstream.WriteLine("    BORDER-BOTTOM: #999 1px solid;");
txtstream.WriteLine("    BACKGROUND-COLOR: #eeeeee;");
txtstream.WriteLine("    FONT-FAMILY: font-family: Cambria, serif;");
txtstream.WriteLine("    FONT-SIZE: 12px;");
txtstream.WriteLine("    text-align: left;");
txtstream.WriteLine("    white-Space: nowrap;");
txtstream.WriteLine("}");
```

```
txtstream.WriteLine("div");
txtstream.WriteLine("{");
txtstream.WriteLine("    BORDER-RIGHT: #999999 3px solid;");
txtstream.WriteLine("    PADDING-RIGHT: 6px;");
txtstream.WriteLine("    PADDING-LEFT: 6px;");
txtstream.WriteLine("    FONT-WEIGHT: Normal;");
txtstream.WriteLine("    PADDING-BOTTOM: 6px;");
txtstream.WriteLine("    COLOR: white;");
txtstream.WriteLine("    PADDING-TOP: 6px;");
txtstream.WriteLine("    BORDER-BOTTOM: #999 1px solid;");
txtstream.WriteLine("    BACKGROUND-COLOR: navy;");
txtstream.WriteLine("    FONT-FAMILY: font-family: Cambria, serif;");
txtstream.WriteLine("    FONT-SIZE: 10px;");
txtstream.WriteLine("    text-align: left;");
txtstream.WriteLine("    white-Space: nowrap;");
txtstream.WriteLine("}");
txtstream.WriteLine("span");
txtstream.WriteLine("{");
txtstream.WriteLine("    BORDER-RIGHT: #999999 3px solid;");
txtstream.WriteLine("    PADDING-RIGHT: 3px;");
txtstream.WriteLine("    PADDING-LEFT: 3px;");
txtstream.WriteLine("    FONT-WEIGHT: Normal;");
txtstream.WriteLine("    PADDING-BOTTOM: 3px;");
txtstream.WriteLine("    COLOR: white;");
txtstream.WriteLine("    PADDING-TOP: 3px;");
txtstream.WriteLine("    BORDER-BOTTOM: #999 1px solid;");
txtstream.WriteLine("    BACKGROUND-COLOR: navy;");
txtstream.WriteLine("  FONT-FAMILY: font-family: Cambria, serif;");
txtstream.WriteLine("    FONT-SIZE: 10px;");
txtstream.WriteLine("    text-align: left;");
txtstream.WriteLine("    white-Space: nowrap;");
txtstream.WriteLine("    display: inline-block;");
txtstream.WriteLine("    width: 100%;");
```

```
txtstream.WriteLine("}");
txtstream.WriteLine("textarea");
txtstream.WriteLine("{");
txtstream.WriteLine("    BORDER-RIGHT: #999999 3px solid;");
txtstream.WriteLine("    PADDING-RIGHT: 3px;");
txtstream.WriteLine("    PADDING-LEFT: 3px;");
txtstream.WriteLine("    FONT-WEIGHT: Normal;");
txtstream.WriteLine("    PADDING-BOTTOM: 3px;");
txtstream.WriteLine("    COLOR: white;");
txtstream.WriteLine("    PADDING-TOP: 3px;");
txtstream.WriteLine("    BORDER-BOTTOM: #999 1px solid;");
txtstream.WriteLine("    BACKGROUND-COLOR: navy;");
txtstream.WriteLine("    FONT-FAMILY: font-family: Cambria, serif;");
txtstream.WriteLine("    FONT-SIZE: 10px;");
txtstream.WriteLine("    text-align: left;");
txtstream.WriteLine("    white-Space: nowrap;");
txtstream.WriteLine("    width: 100%;");
txtstream.WriteLine("}");
txtstream.WriteLine("select");
txtstream.WriteLine("{");
txtstream.WriteLine("    BORDER-RIGHT: #999999 3px solid;");
txtstream.WriteLine("    PADDING-RIGHT: 6px;");
txtstream.WriteLine("    PADDING-LEFT: 6px;");
txtstream.WriteLine("    FONT-WEIGHT: Normal;");
txtstream.WriteLine("    PADDING-BOTTOM: 6px;");
txtstream.WriteLine("    COLOR: white;");
txtstream.WriteLine("    PADDING-TOP: 6px;");
txtstream.WriteLine("    BORDER-BOTTOM: #999 1px solid;");
txtstream.WriteLine("    BACKGROUND-COLOR: navy;");
txtstream.WriteLine("    FONT-FAMILY: font-family: Cambria, serif;");
txtstream.WriteLine("    FONT-SIZE: 10px;");
txtstream.WriteLine("    text-align: left;");
txtstream.WriteLine("    white-Space: nowrap;");
```

```
txtstream.WriteLine("    width: 100%;");
txtstream.WriteLine("}");
txtstream.WriteLine("input");
txtstream.WriteLine("{");
txtstream.WriteLine("    BORDER-RIGHT: #999999 3px solid;");
txtstream.WriteLine("    PADDING-RIGHT: 3px;");
txtstream.WriteLine("    PADDING-LEFT: 3px;");
txtstream.WriteLine("    FONT-WEIGHT: Bold;");
txtstream.WriteLine("    PADDING-BOTTOM: 3px;");
txtstream.WriteLine("    COLOR: white;");
txtstream.WriteLine("    PADDING-TOP: 3px;");
txtstream.WriteLine("    BORDER-BOTTOM: #999 1px solid;");
txtstream.WriteLine("    BACKGROUND-COLOR: navy;");
txtstream.WriteLine("    FONT-FAMILY: font-family: Cambria, serif;");
txtstream.WriteLine("    FONT-SIZE: 12px;");
txtstream.WriteLine("    text-align: left;");
txtstream.WriteLine("    display: table-cell;");
txtstream.WriteLine("    white-Space: nowrap;");
txtstream.WriteLine("    width: 100%;");
txtstream.WriteLine("}");
txtstream.WriteLine("h1 {");
txtstream.WriteLine("color: antiquewhite;");
txtstream.WriteLine("text-shadow: 1px 1px 1px black;");
txtstream.WriteLine("padding: 3px;");
txtstream.WriteLine("text-align: center;");
txtstream.WriteLine("box-shadow: inset 2px 2px 5px rgba(0,0,0,0.5), inset -2px -2px 5px rgba(255,255,255,0.5)");
txtstream.WriteLine("}");
txtstream.WriteLine("</style>");
txtstream.WriteLine("</head>");
txtstream.WriteLine("<body>");
txtstream.WriteLine("<table        Border='1'        cellpadding='1' cellspacing='1'>");
```

```
switch (Orientation)
{


    case "Single-Line Horizontal":
        {
            for (var y = 0; y < Rows.Count; y++)
            {
                txtstream.WriteLine("<tr>");
                for (var x = 0; x < Names.Count; x++)
                {
                    txtstream.WriteLine("<th>" + Names(x) + "</th>");
                }
                txtstream.WriteLine("</tr>");
                txtstream.WriteLine("<tr>");
                for (var x = 0; x < Names.Count; x++)
                {
                    String value = Rows(y)(x);
                    txtstream.WriteLine("<td>" + value + "</td>");
                }
                txtstream.WriteLine("</tr>");
                break;
            }
            break;
        }

    case "Multi-Line Horizontal":
        {

            for (var y = 0; y < Rows.Count; y++)
            {
```

```
                      txtstream.WriteLine("<tr>");
                      for (var x = 0; x < Names.Count; x++)
                      {
                          txtstream.WriteLine("<th>" + Names(x) + "</th>");
                      }
                      txtstream.WriteLine("</tr>");
                      break;
                  }
                  for (var y = 0; y < Rows.Count; y++)
                  {
                      txtstream.WriteLine("<tr>");
                      for (var x = 0; x < Names.Count; x++)
                      {
                          string value = Rows(y)(x);
                          txtstream.WriteLine("<td>" + value + "</td>");
                      }
                      txtstream.WriteLine("</tr>");
                  }
                  break;
              }
          case "Single-Line Vertical":
              {

                  for (var y = 0; y < Rows.Count; y++)
                  {

                      for (var x = 0; x < Names.Count; x++)
                      {
                          txtstream.WriteLine("<tr><th>" + Names(x) + "</th><td>"
+ Rows(y)(x) + "</td></tr>");
                      }
                      break;
                  }
```

```
            break;
        }

    case "Multi-Line Vertical":
        {

            for (var x = 0; x < Names.Count; x++)
            {

                txtstream.WriteLine("<tr><th>" + Names(x) + "</th>“);
                for (var y = 0; y < Rows.Count; y++)
                {
                    string value = Rows(y)(x);
                    txtstream.WriteLine("<td>" + value + "</td>“);
                }
                txtstream.WriteLine("</tr>“);
            }
            break;
        }
}
txtstream.WriteLine("</table>“);
txtstream.WriteLine("</body>“);
txtstream.WriteLine("</html>“);
txtstream.Close();
```

CREATE HTML CODE

Inside this sub routine is the code to create an HTML Webpage that can be saved and displayed using the Web Browser control or saved and displayed at a later time.

```
var ws = new ActiveXObject("WScript.Shell");
var fso = new ActiveXObject("Scripting.FileSystemObject");
txtstream = fso.OpenTextFile(ws.CurrentDirectory + "\\Process.asp", 2,
true, -2);

txtstream.WriteLine("<html>");
txtstream.WriteLine("<head>");
txtstream.WriteLine("<title>Win32_Process</title>");
txtstream.WriteLine("<style type='text/css'>");
txtstream.WriteLine("body");
txtstream.WriteLine("{");
txtstream.WriteLine("   PADDING-RIGHT: 0px;");
txtstream.WriteLine("   PADDING-LEFT: 0px;");
txtstream.WriteLine("   PADDING-BOTTOM: 0px;");
txtstream.WriteLine("   MARGIN: 0px;");
txtstream.WriteLine("   COLOR: #333;");
txtstream.WriteLine("   PADDING-TOP: 0px;");
txtstream.WriteLine("    FONT-FAMILY: verdana, arial, helvetica, sans-
serif;");
txtstream.WriteLine("}");
txtstream.WriteLine("table");
txtstream.WriteLine("{");
txtstream.WriteLine("   BORDER-RIGHT: #999999 1px solid;");
```

```
txtstream.WriteLine("   PADDING-RIGHT: 1px;");
txtstream.WriteLine("   PADDING-LEFT: 1px;");
txtstream.WriteLine("   PADDING-BOTTOM: 1px;");
txtstream.WriteLine("   LINE-HEIGHT: 8px;");
txtstream.WriteLine("   PADDING-TOP: 1px;");
txtstream.WriteLine("   BORDER-BOTTOM: #999 1px solid;");
txtstream.WriteLine("   BACKGROUND-COLOR: #eeeeee;");
txtstream.WriteLine("
filter:progid:DXImageTransform.Microsoft.Shadow(color='silver',     Direction=135,
Strength=16)");
txtstream.WriteLine("}");
txtstream.WriteLine("th");
txtstream.WriteLine("{");
txtstream.WriteLine("   BORDER-RIGHT: #999999 3px solid;");
txtstream.WriteLine("   PADDING-RIGHT: 6px;");
txtstream.WriteLine("   PADDING-LEFT: 6px;");
txtstream.WriteLine("   FONT-WEIGHT: Bold;");
txtstream.WriteLine("   FONT-SIZE: 14px;");
txtstream.WriteLine("   PADDING-BOTTOM: 6px;");
txtstream.WriteLine("   COLOR: darkred;");
txtstream.WriteLine("   LINE-HEIGHT: 14px;");
txtstream.WriteLine("   PADDING-TOP: 6px;");
txtstream.WriteLine("   BORDER-BOTTOM: #999 1px solid;");
txtstream.WriteLine("   BACKGROUND-COLOR: #eeeeee;");
txtstream.WriteLine("   FONT-FAMILY: font-family: Cambria, serif;");
txtstream.WriteLine("   FONT-SIZE: 12px;");
txtstream.WriteLine("   text-align: left;");
txtstream.WriteLine("   white-Space: nowrap;");
txtstream.WriteLine("}");
txtstream.WriteLine(".th");
txtstream.WriteLine("{");
txtstream.WriteLine("   BORDER-RIGHT: #999999 2px solid;");
txtstream.WriteLine("   PADDING-RIGHT: 6px;");
```

```
txtstream.WriteLine("    PADDING-LEFT: 6px;");
txtstream.WriteLine("    FONT-WEIGHT: Bold;");
txtstream.WriteLine("    PADDING-BOTTOM: 6px;");
txtstream.WriteLine("    COLOR: black;");
txtstream.WriteLine("    PADDING-TOP: 6px;");
txtstream.WriteLine("    BORDER-BOTTOM: #999 2px solid;");
txtstream.WriteLine("    BACKGROUND-COLOR: #eeeeee;");
txtstream.WriteLine("    FONT-FAMILY: font-family: Cambria, serif;");
txtstream.WriteLine("    FONT-SIZE: 10px;");
txtstream.WriteLine("    text-align: right;");
txtstream.WriteLine("    white-Space: nowrap;");
txtstream.WriteLine("}");
txtstream.WriteLine("td");
txtstream.WriteLine("{");
txtstream.WriteLine("    BORDER-RIGHT: #999999 3px solid;");
txtstream.WriteLine("    PADDING-RIGHT: 6px;");
txtstream.WriteLine("    PADDING-LEFT: 6px;");
txtstream.WriteLine("    FONT-WEIGHT: Normal;");
txtstream.WriteLine("    PADDING-BOTTOM: 6px;");
txtstream.WriteLine("    COLOR: navy;");
txtstream.WriteLine("    LINE-HEIGHT: 14px;");
txtstream.WriteLine("    PADDING-TOP: 6px;");
txtstream.WriteLine("    BORDER-BOTTOM: #999 1px solid;");
txtstream.WriteLine("    BACKGROUND-COLOR: #eeeeee;");
txtstream.WriteLine("    FONT-FAMILY: font-family: Cambria, serif;");
txtstream.WriteLine("    FONT-SIZE: 12px;");
txtstream.WriteLine("    text-align: left;");
txtstream.WriteLine("    white-Space: nowrap;");
txtstream.WriteLine("}");
txtstream.WriteLine("div");
txtstream.WriteLine("{");
txtstream.WriteLine("    BORDER-RIGHT: #999999 3px solid;");
txtstream.WriteLine("    PADDING-RIGHT: 6px;");
```

```
txtstream.WriteLine("   PADDING-LEFT: 6px;");
txtstream.WriteLine("   FONT-WEIGHT: Normal;");
txtstream.WriteLine("   PADDING-BOTTOM: 6px;");
txtstream.WriteLine("   COLOR: white;");
txtstream.WriteLine("   PADDING-TOP: 6px;");
txtstream.WriteLine("   BORDER-BOTTOM: #999 1px solid;");
txtstream.WriteLine("   BACKGROUND-COLOR: navy;");
txtstream.WriteLine("   FONT-FAMILY: font-family: Cambria, serif;");
txtstream.WriteLine("   FONT-SIZE: 10px;");
txtstream.WriteLine("   text-align: left;");
txtstream.WriteLine("   white-Space: nowrap;");
txtstream.WriteLine("}");
txtstream.WriteLine("span");
txtstream.WriteLine("{");
txtstream.WriteLine("   BORDER-RIGHT: #999999 3px solid;");
txtstream.WriteLine("   PADDING-RIGHT: 3px;");
txtstream.WriteLine("   PADDING-LEFT: 3px;");
txtstream.WriteLine("   FONT-WEIGHT: Normal;");
txtstream.WriteLine("   PADDING-BOTTOM: 3px;");
txtstream.WriteLine("   COLOR: white;");
txtstream.WriteLine("   PADDING-TOP: 3px;");
txtstream.WriteLine("   BORDER-BOTTOM: #999 1px solid;");
txtstream.WriteLine("   BACKGROUND-COLOR: navy;");
txtstream.WriteLine("   FONT-FAMILY: font-family: Cambria, serif;");
txtstream.WriteLine("   FONT-SIZE: 10px;");
txtstream.WriteLine("   text-align: left;");
txtstream.WriteLine("   white-Space: nowrap;");
txtstream.WriteLine("   display: inline-block;");
txtstream.WriteLine("   width: 100%;");
txtstream.WriteLine("}");
txtstream.WriteLine("textarea");
txtstream.WriteLine("{");
txtstream.WriteLine("   BORDER-RIGHT: #999999 3px solid;");
```

```
txtstream.WriteLine("    PADDING-RIGHT: 3px;");
txtstream.WriteLine("    PADDING-LEFT: 3px;");
txtstream.WriteLine("    FONT-WEIGHT: Normal;");
txtstream.WriteLine("    PADDING-BOTTOM: 3px;");
txtstream.WriteLine("    COLOR: white;");
txtstream.WriteLine("    PADDING-TOP: 3px;");
txtstream.WriteLine("    BORDER-BOTTOM: #999 1px solid;");
txtstream.WriteLine("    BACKGROUND-COLOR: navy;");
txtstream.WriteLine("    FONT-FAMILY: font-family: Cambria, serif;");
txtstream.WriteLine("    FONT-SIZE: 10px;");
txtstream.WriteLine("    text-align: left;");
txtstream.WriteLine("    white-Space: nowrap;");
txtstream.WriteLine("    width: 100%;");
txtstream.WriteLine("}");
txtstream.WriteLine("select");
txtstream.WriteLine("{");
txtstream.WriteLine("    BORDER-RIGHT: #999999 3px solid;");
txtstream.WriteLine("    PADDING-RIGHT: 6px;");
txtstream.WriteLine("    PADDING-LEFT: 6px;");
txtstream.WriteLine("    FONT-WEIGHT: Normal;");
txtstream.WriteLine("    PADDING-BOTTOM: 6px;");
txtstream.WriteLine("    COLOR: white;");
txtstream.WriteLine("    PADDING-TOP: 6px;");
txtstream.WriteLine("    BORDER-BOTTOM: #999 1px solid;");
txtstream.WriteLine("    BACKGROUND-COLOR: navy;");
txtstream.WriteLine("    FONT-FAMILY: font-family: Cambria, serif;");
txtstream.WriteLine("    FONT-SIZE: 10px;");
txtstream.WriteLine("    text-align: left;");
txtstream.WriteLine("    white-Space: nowrap;");
txtstream.WriteLine("    width: 100%;");
txtstream.WriteLine("}");
txtstream.WriteLine("input");
txtstream.WriteLine("{");
```

```
txtstream.WriteLine("    BORDER-RIGHT: #999999 3px solid;");
txtstream.WriteLine("    PADDING-RIGHT: 3px;");
txtstream.WriteLine("    PADDING-LEFT: 3px;");
txtstream.WriteLine("    FONT-WEIGHT: Bold;");
txtstream.WriteLine("    PADDING-BOTTOM: 3px;");
txtstream.WriteLine("    COLOR: white;");
txtstream.WriteLine("    PADDING-TOP: 3px;");
txtstream.WriteLine("    BORDER-BOTTOM: #999 1px solid;");
txtstream.WriteLine("    BACKGROUND-COLOR: navy;");
txtstream.WriteLine("    FONT-FAMILY: font-family: Cambria, serif;");
txtstream.WriteLine("    FONT-SIZE: 12px;");
txtstream.WriteLine("    text-align: left;");
txtstream.WriteLine("    display: table-cell;");
txtstream.WriteLine("    white-Space: nowrap;");
txtstream.WriteLine("    width: 100%;");
txtstream.WriteLine("}");
txtstream.WriteLine("h1 {");
txtstream.WriteLine("color: antiquewhite;");
txtstream.WriteLine("text-shadow: 1px 1px 1px black;");
txtstream.WriteLine("padding: 3px;");
txtstream.WriteLine("text-align: center;");
txtstream.WriteLine("box-shadow: inset 2px 2px 5px rgba(0,0,0,0.5),
inset -2px -2px 5px rgba(255,255,255,0.5)");
txtstream.WriteLine("}");
txtstream.WriteLine("</style>");
txtstream.WriteLine("</head>");
txtstream.WriteLine("<body>");
txtstream.WriteLine("<table          Border='1'          cellpadding='1'
cellspacing='1'>");


switch (Orientation)
{
```

```
case "Single-Line Horizontal":
{
    for (var y = 0; y < Rows.Count; y++)
    {
        txtstream.WriteLine("<tr>");
        for (var x = 0; x < Names.Count; x++)
        {
            txtstream.WriteLine("<th>" + Names(x) + "</th>");
        }
        txtstream.WriteLine("</tr>");
        txtstream.WriteLine("<tr>");
        for (var x = 0; x < Names.Count; x++)
        {
            String value = Rows(y)(x);
            txtstream.WriteLine("<td>" + value + "</td>");
        }
        txtstream.WriteLine("</tr>");
        break;
    }
    break;
}

case "Multi-Line Horizontal":
{

    for (var y = 0; y < Rows.Count; y++)
    {
        txtstream.WriteLine("<tr>");
        for (var x = 0; x < Names.Count; x++)
        {
            txtstream.WriteLine("<th>" + Names(x) + "</th>");
```

```
            }
            txtstream.WriteLine("</tr>");
            break;
          }
          for (var y = 0; y < Rows.Count; y++)
          {
            txtstream.WriteLine("<tr>");
            for (var x = 0; x < Names.Count; x++)
            {
              string value = Rows(y)(x);
              txtstream.WriteLine("<td>" + value + "</td>");
            }
            txtstream.WriteLine("</tr>");
          }
          break;
        }
      case "Single-Line Vertical":
        {

          for (var y = 0; y < Rows.Count; y++)
          {

            for (var x = 0; x < Names.Count; x++)
            {
              txtstream.WriteLine("<tr><th>" + Names(x) + "</th><td>"
+ Rows(y)(x) + "</td></tr>");
            }
            break;
          }
          break;
        }

      case "Multi-Line Vertical":
```

```
{

    for (var x = 0; x < Names.Count; x++)
    {

        txtstream.WriteLine("<tr><th>" + Names(x) + "</th>");
        for (var y = 0; y < Rows.Count; y++)
        {
            string value = Rows(y)(x);
            txtstream.WriteLine("<td>" + value + "</td>");
        }
        txtstream.WriteLine("</tr>");
    }
    break;
    }

}
txtstream.WriteLine("</table>");
txtstream.WriteLine("</body>");
txtstream.WriteLine("</html>");
txtstream.Close();
```

CREATE THE CSV FILE

Inside this sub routine is the code to create a CSV file. It is a separate routine because its extension -.csv – is seen by Excel – assuming it is installed as a text-based data file and knows what to do with it to display its contents.

```
String tempstr = "";
var ws = new ActiveXObject("WScript.Shell");
var fso = new ActiveXObject("Scripting.FileSystemObject");
txtstream = fso.OpenTextFile(ws.CurrentDirectory + "\\Process.csv", 2,
true, -2);

switch (Orientation)
{

    case "Single-Line Horizontal":
        {

            for (var x = 0; x < Names.Count; x++)
            {
              if (tempstr != "");
              {
                 tempstr = tempstr + ",";


              }
              tempstr = tempstr + Names(x);


            }
            txtstream.WriteLine(tempstr);
            tempstr = "";
```

```
for (var y = 0; y < Rows.Count; y++)
{
    for (var x = 0; x < Names.Count; x++)
    {
        if (tempstr != ""“);
        {
            tempstr = tempstr + ",";
        }
        tempstr = tempstr + '''' + Rows(y)(x) + '''';

    }
    txtstream.WriteLine(tempstr);
    tempstr = "";

}
txtstream.Close();

break;
}
case "Vertical":
{

    for (var x = 0; x < Names.Count; x++)
    {
        tempstr = Names(x);
        for (var y = 0; y < Rows.Count; y++)
        {

            if (tempstr != ""“);
            {
                tempstr = tempstr + ",";
            }
            tempstr = tempstr + (char)34 + Rows(y)(x) + (char)34;
```

```
            }
            txtstream.WriteLine(tempstr);
            tempstr = "";
          }
        break;


      }
    }
```

CREATE THE EXCEL FILE

Inside this sub routine is the code to create a CSV file and then open it using an older version of Excel.

```
String tempstr = "";
var ws = new ActiveXObject("WScript.Shell");
var fso = new ActiveXObject("Scripting.FileSystemObject");
txtstream = fso.OpenTextFile(ws.CurrentDirectory + "\\Process.csv", 2,
true, -2);

switch (Orientation)
{

    case "Single-Line Horizontal":
      {

          for (var x = 0; x < Names.Count; x++)
          {
            if (tempstr != "");
            {

                tempstr = tempstr + ",";

            }
            tempstr = tempstr + Names(x);

          }
          txtstream.WriteLine(tempstr);
          tempstr = "";
```

```
for (var y = 0; y < Rows.Count; y++)
{
    for (var x = 0; x < Names.Count; x++)
    {
        if (tempstr != "");
        {
            tempstr = tempstr + ",";
        }
        tempstr = tempstr + '"' + Rows(y)(x) + '"';

    }
    txtstream.WriteLine(tempstr);
    tempstr = "";

}
txtstream.Close();

break;
}
case "Vertical":
{

    for (var x = 0; x < Names.Count; x++)
    {
        tempstr = Names(x);
        for (var y = 0; y < Rows.Count; y++)
        {

            if (tempstr != "");
            {
                tempstr = tempstr + ",";
            }
```

```
                tempstr = tempstr + (char)34 + Rows(y)(x) + (char)34;

            }
            txtstream.WriteLine(tempstr);
            tempstr = "";
        }
        break;
    }
}
```

EXCEL AUTOMATION CODE

Inside this sub routine is the code to create an instance of Excel and populate a worksheet. Both horizontal and vertical orientations are available, and the code automatically aligns and autofits the cells.

```
var oExcel = new ActiveXObject("Excel.Application");
var wb = oExcel.Workbooks.Add();
var ws = wb.Worksheets(0);
switch (Orientation)
{

    case "Horizontal":
        {
            for (var x = 0; x < Names.Count; x++)
            {
                ws.Cells(1, x + 1) = Names(x);
            }
            for (var y = 0; y < Rows.Count; y++)
            {
                for (var x = 0; x < Names.Count; x++)
                {
                    ws.Cells(y + 2, x + 1) = Rows(y)(x);
                }
            }
            break;
        }
    case "Vertical":
        {
            for (var x = 0; x < Names.Count; x++)
            {
                ws.Cells(x + 1, 1) = Names(x);
            }
            for (var y = 0; y < Rows.Count; y++)
            {
```

```
        for (var x = 0; x < Names.Count; x++)
        {
            ws.Cells(x + 1, y + 2) = Rows(y)(x);
        }
    }
    break;
}
}
ws.Columns.HorizontalAlignment = -3141
ws.Columns.AutoFit();
```

CREATE CUSTOM DELIMITED TEXT FILE

This sub routine is designed to provide you with maximum flexibility. You choose the orientation and the delimiter.

```
String tempstr = "";
var ws = new ActiveXObject("WScript.Shell");
var fso = new ActiveXObject("Scripting.FileSystemObject");
txtstream = fso.OpenTextFile(ws.CurrentDirectory + "\\Process.txt", 2,
true, -2);

switch (Orientation)
{

    case "Single-Line Horizontal":
        {

            for (var x = 0; x < Names.Count; x++)
            {
              if (tempstr != "");
              {
                  tempstr = tempstr + Delim;

              }
              tempstr = tempstr + Names(x);
```

```
                }
            txtstream.WriteLine(tempstr);
            tempstr = "";

            for (var y = 0; y < Rows.Count; y++)
            {
                for (var x = 0; x < Names.Count; x++)
                {
                    if (tempstr != "");
                    {
                        tempstr = tempstr + Delim;
                    }
                    tempstr = tempstr + '"' + Rows(y)(x) + '"';

                }
                txtstream.WriteLine(tempstr);
                tempstr = "";

            }
            txtstream.Close();

            break;
        }
    case "Vertical":
        {

            for (var x = 0; x < Names.Count; x++)
            {
                tempstr = Names(x);
                for (var y = 0; y < Rows.Count; y++)
                {

                    if (tempstr != "");
```

```
            {
                tempstr = tempstr + Delim;
            }
            tempstr = tempstr + (char)34 + Rows(y)(x) + (char)34;

        }
        txtstream.WriteLine(tempstr);
        tempstr = "";
    }
    break;


}
}
```

CREATE AN EXCEL SPREADSHEET TEXT FILE

Simply put, this routine creates an Excel Spreadsheet File that will automatically be displayed by Excel as a worksheet.

```
var ws = new ActiveXObject("WScript.Shell");
var fso = new ActiveXObject("Scripting.FileSystemObject");
txtstream = fso.OpenTextFile(ws.CurrentDirectory + "\\Process.xml", 2, true, -2);

txtstream.WriteLine("<?xml version='1.0'?>");
txtstream.WriteLine("<?mso-application progid='Excel.Sheet'?>");
txtstream.WriteLine("<Workbook       xmlns='urn:schemas-microsoft-com:office:spreadsheet'       xmlns:o='urn:schemas-microsoft-com:office:office' xmlns:x='urn:schemas-microsoft-com:office:excel'       xmlns:ss='urn:schemas-microsoft-com:office:spreadsheet'       xmlns:html='http://www.w3.org/TR/REC-html40'>");
txtstream.WriteLine("    <Documentproperties  xmlns='urn:schemas-microsoft-com:office:office'>");
txtstream.WriteLine("    <Author>Windows User</Author>");
txtstream.WriteLine("    <LastAuthor>Windows User</LastAuthor>");
txtstream.WriteLine("        <Created>2007-11-27T19:36:16Z</Created>");
txtstream.WriteLine("    <Version>12.00</Version>");
```

```
txtstream.WriteLine("    </Documentproperties>");
txtstream.WriteLine("              <ExcelWorkbook    xmlns='urn:schemas-
microsoft-com:office:excel'>");
txtstream.WriteLine("      <WindowHeight>11835</WindowHeight>");
txtstream.WriteLine("      <WindowWidth>18960</WindowWidth>");
txtstream.WriteLine("      <WindowTopX>120</WindowTopX>");
txtstream.WriteLine("      <WindowTopY>135</WindowTopY>");
txtstream.WriteLine("
<ProtectStructure>False</ProtectStructure>");
txtstream.WriteLine("
<ProtectWindows>False</ProtectWindows>");
txtstream.WriteLine("    </ExcelWorkbook>");
txtstream.WriteLine("    <Styles>");
txtstream.WriteLine("      <Style ss:ID='Default' ss:Name='Normal'>");
txtstream.WriteLine("        <Alignment ss:Vertical='Bottom'/>");
txtstream.WriteLine("        <Borders/>");
txtstream.WriteLine("                    <Font   ss:FontName='Calibri'
x:Family='Swiss' ss:Size='11' ss:Color='#000000'/>");
txtstream.WriteLine("        <Varerior/>");
txtstream.WriteLine("        <NumberFormat/>");
txtstream.WriteLine("        <Protection/>");
txtstream.WriteLine("      </Style>");
txtstream.WriteLine("      <Style ss:ID='s62'>");
txtstream.WriteLine("        <Borders/>");
txtstream.WriteLine("                    <Font   ss:FontName='Calibri'
x:Family='Swiss' ss:Size='11' ss:Color='#000000' ss:Bold='1'/>");
txtstream.WriteLine("      </Style>");
txtstream.WriteLine("      <Style ss:ID='s63'>");
txtstream.WriteLine("                    <Alignment  ss:Horizontal='Left'
ss:Vertical='Bottom' ss:Indent='2'/>");
txtstream.WriteLine("                    <Font   ss:FontName='Verdana'
x:Family='Swiss' ss:Size='7.7' ss:Color='#000000'/>");
txtstream.WriteLine("      </Style>");
```

```
txtstream.WriteLine("   </Styles>");
txtstream.WriteLine("<Worksheet ss:Name='Process'>");
txtstream.WriteLine("        <Table   x:FullColumns='1'   x:FullRows='1'
ss:DefaultRowHeight='24.9375'>");
txtstream.WriteLine("      <Column ss:AutoFitWidth='1' ss:Width='82.5'
ss:Span='5'/>");
txtstream.WriteLine("     <Row ss:AutoFitHeight='0'>");
for (var x = 0; x < Names.Count; x++)
{
    txtstream.WriteLine("                    <Cell  ss:StyleID='s62'><Data
ss:Type='String'>" + Names(x) + "</Data></Cell>");
}
txtstream.WriteLine("     </Row>");
for (var y = 0; y < Rows.Count; y++)
{
    txtstream.WriteLine("                   <Row    ss:AutoFitHeight='0'
ss:Height='13.5'>");
    for (var x = 0; x < Names.Count; x++)
    {
        txtstream.WriteLine("                          <Cell><Data
ss:Type='String'><![CDATA(" + Rows(y)(x) + "))></Data></Cell>");
    }
    txtstream.WriteLine("     </Row>");
}
txtstream.WriteLine("  </Table>");
txtstream.WriteLine("        <WorksheetOptions   xmlns='urn:schemas-
microsoft-com:office:excel'>");
txtstream.WriteLine("    <PageSetup>");
txtstream.WriteLine("     <Header x:Margin='0.3'/>");
txtstream.WriteLine("     <Footer x:Margin='0.3'/>");
txtstream.WriteLine("        <PageMargins x:Bottom='0.75' x:Left='0.7'
x:Right='0.7' x:Top='0.75'/>");
txtstream.WriteLine("    </PageSetup>");
```

```
        txtstream.WriteLine("    <Unsynced/>");
        txtstream.WriteLine("    <Prvar>");
        txtstream.WriteLine("      <FitHeight>0</FitHeight>");
        txtstream.WriteLine("      <ValidPrvarerInfo/>");
        txtstream.WriteLine("
<HorizontalResolution>600</HorizontalResolution>");
        txtstream.WriteLine("
<VerticalResolution>600</VerticalResolution>");
        txtstream.WriteLine("    </Prvar>");
        txtstream.WriteLine("    <Selected/>");
        txtstream.WriteLine("    <Panes>");
        txtstream.WriteLine("     <Pane>");
        txtstream.WriteLine("       <Number>3</Number>");
        txtstream.WriteLine("        <ActiveRow>9</ActiveRow>");
        txtstream.WriteLine("        <ActiveCol>7</ActiveCol>");
        txtstream.WriteLine("     </Pane>");
        txtstream.WriteLine("    </Panes>");
        txtstream.WriteLine("    <ProtectObjects>False</ProtectObjects>");
        txtstream.WriteLine("
<ProtectScenarios>False</ProtectScenarios>");
        txtstream.WriteLine("  </WorksheetOptions>");
        txtstream.WriteLine("</Worksheet>");
        txtstream.WriteLine("</Workbook>");
        txtstream.Close();

    }
```

CREATE AN XML FILE

This sub routine creates a very simple Element XML File. This file can be used with the MSDAOSP and therefore, becomes as database text file.

```
var ws = new ActiveXObject("WScript.Shell");
var fso = new ActiveXObject("Scripting.FileSystemObject");
txtstream = fso.OpenTextFile(ws.CurrentDirectory + "\\Process.xml", 2,
true, -2);

txtstream.WriteLine("<?xml version='1.0' encoding='iso-8859-1'?>");
txtstream.WriteLine("<data>");
for (var y = 0; y < Rows.Count; y++)
{
   txtstream.WriteLine("<Win32_process>");
   for (var x = 0; x < Names.Count; x++)
   {
      txtstream.WriteLine("<" + Names(x) + ">" + Rows(y)(x) + "</" +
Names(x) + ">");
   }
   txtstream.WriteLine("</Win32_process>");
}
txtstream.WriteLine("</data>");
txtstream.Close();
```

CREATE XML FOR XSL FILE

```
var ws = new ActiveXObject("WScript.Shell");
var fso = new ActiveXObject("Scripting.FileSystemObject");
txtstream = fso.OpenTextFile(ws.CurrentDirectory + "\\Process.xml", 2, true, -2);
txtstream.WriteLine("<?xml version='1.0' encoding='iso-8859-1'?>");
txtstream.WriteLine("<?xml-stylesheet    type='Text/xsl'    href='" + Ws.CurrentDirectory + "\\Win32_Process.xsl'?>");
txtstream.WriteLine("<data>");
for (var y = 0; y < Rows.Count; y++)
{
    txtstream.WriteLine("<Win32_process>");
    for (var x = 0; x < Names.Count; x++)
    {
        txtstream.WriteLine("<" + Names(x) + ">" + Rows(y)(x) + "</" + Names(x) + ">");
    }
    txtstream.WriteLine("</Win32_process>");
}
txtstream.WriteLine("</data>");
txtstream.Close();
```

CREATE A SCHEMA XML

This sub routine creates a very simple Element XML File but is dependent upon the specified XSL file. It is opened by ADO and uses the MSDAOSP provider.

This file is then saved and can be used by the MSPERSIST provider.

```javascript
var ws = new ActiveXObject("WScript.Shell");
var fso = new ActiveXObject("Scripting.FileSystemObject");
txtstream = fso.OpenTextFile(ws.CurrentDirectory + "\\Process.xml", 2, true, -2);

txtstream.WriteLine("<?xml version='1.0' encoding='iso-8859-1'?>");
txtstream.WriteLine("<data>");
for (var y = 0; y < Rows.Count; y++)
{
    txtstream.WriteLine("<Win32_process>");
    for (var x = 0; x < Names.Count; x++)
    {
        txtstream.WriteLine("<" + Names(x) + ">" + Rows(y)(x) + "</" + Names(x) + ">");
    }
    txtstream.WriteLine("</Win32_process>");
}
txtstream.WriteLine("</data>");
txtstream.Close();
```

```
ADODB.Recordset rs1 = new ADODB.Recordset();
rs1.ActiveConnection          =         "Provider=MSDAOSP;          Data
Source=msxml2.DSOControl";
rs1.Open(Ws.CurrentDirectory + "\\Win32_Process.xml");


if                (fso.FileExists(Ws.CurrentDirectory                +
"\\Win32_Process_Schema.xml"); == true)
{
    fso.DeleteFile(Ws.CurrentDirectory                          +
"\\Win32_Process_Schema.xml");
}
rs1.Save(Ws.CurrentDirectory + "\\Win32_Process_Schema.xml", 1);
```

CREATE THE XSL FILES

Inside this sub routine is the code to create the XSL File designed to render the XML as an HTML Webpage. It can be saved and displayed using the Web Browser control or saved and displayed at a later time. Simply pass in the collection generated by the Return_Management_Collection and specify its orientation.

```
var ws = new ActiveXObject("WScript.Shell");
var fso = new ActiveXObject("Scripting.FileSystemObject");
txtstream = fso.OpenTextFile(ws.CurrentDirectory + "\\Process.xml", 2,
true, -2);

switch (Orientation)
{

    case "Single-Line Horizontal":
      {
        txtstream.WriteLine("<?xml       version='1.0'    encoding='UTF-
8'?>");
        txtstream.WriteLine("<xsl:stylesheet                version='1.0'
xmlns:xsl='http://www.w3.org/1999/XSL/Transform'>");
        txtstream.WriteLine("<xsl:template match=\"/\">");
        txtstream.WriteLine("<html>");
        txtstream.WriteLine("<head>");
        txtstream.WriteLine("<title>Products</title>");
        txtstream.WriteLine("<style type='text/css'>");
        txtstream.WriteLine("th");
```

```
txtstream.WriteLine("{");
txtstream.WriteLine("   COLOR: darkred;");
txtstream.WriteLine("   BACKGROUND-COLOR: white;");
txtstream.WriteLine("    FONT-FAMILY:font-family: Cambria, serif;");

txtstream.WriteLine("   FONT-SIZE: 12px;");
txtstream.WriteLine("   text-align: left;");
txtstream.WriteLine("   white-Space: nowrap;");
txtstream.WriteLine("}");
txtstream.WriteLine("td");
txtstream.WriteLine("{");
txtstream.WriteLine("   COLOR: navy;");
txtstream.WriteLine("   BACKGROUND-COLOR: white;");
txtstream.WriteLine("    FONT-FAMILY: font-family: Cambria, serif;");

txtstream.WriteLine("   FONT-SIZE: 12px;");
txtstream.WriteLine("   text-align: left;");
txtstream.WriteLine("   white-Space: nowrap;");
txtstream.WriteLine("}");
txtstream.WriteLine("</style>");
txtstream.WriteLine("</head>");
txtstream.WriteLine("<body bgcolor='#333333'>");
txtstream.WriteLine("<table colspacing='3' colpadding='3'>");
txtstream.WriteLine("<tr>");
for (var x = 0; x < Names.Count; x++)
{
   txtstream.WriteLine("<th>" + Names(x) + "</th>");
}
txtstream.WriteLine("</tr>");
txtstream.WriteLine("<tr>");
for (var x = 0; x < Names.Count; x++)
{
```

```
                txtstream.WriteLine("<td><xsl:value-of
select=\"data/Win32_Process/" + Names(x) + "\"/></td>");
                }
                txtstream.WriteLine("</tr>");
                txtstream.WriteLine("</table>");
                txtstream.WriteLine("</body>");
                txtstream.WriteLine("</html>");
                txtstream.WriteLine("</xsl:template>");
                txtstream.WriteLine("</xsl:stylesheet>");
                txtstream.Close();

                break;
            }
        case "Multi Line Horizontal":
            {

                txtstream.WriteLine("<?xml    version='1.0'    encoding='UTF-
8'?>");
                txtstream.WriteLine("<xsl:stylesheet             version='1.0'
xmlns:xsl='http://www.w3.org/1999/XSL/Transform'>");
                txtstream.WriteLine("<xsl:template match=\"/\">");
                txtstream.WriteLine("<html>");
                txtstream.WriteLine("<head>");
                txtstream.WriteLine("<title>Products</title>");
                txtstream.WriteLine("<style type='text/css'>");
                txtstream.WriteLine("th");
                txtstream.WriteLine("{");
                txtstream.WriteLine("   COLOR: darkred;");
                txtstream.WriteLine("   BACKGROUND-COLOR: white;");
                txtstream.WriteLine("      FONT-FAMILY:font-family: Cambria,
serif;");
                txtstream.WriteLine("   FONT-SIZE: 12px;");
                txtstream.WriteLine("   text-align: left;");
```

```
            txtstream.WriteLine("   white-Space: nowrap;");
            txtstream.WriteLine("}");
            txtstream.WriteLine("td");
            txtstream.WriteLine("{");
            txtstream.WriteLine("   COLOR: navy;");
            txtstream.WriteLine("   BACKGROUND-COLOR: white;");
            txtstream.WriteLine("    FONT-FAMILY: font-family: Cambria,
serif;");
            txtstream.WriteLine("   FONT-SIZE: 12px;");
            txtstream.WriteLine("   text-align: left;");
            txtstream.WriteLine("   white-Space: nowrap;");
            txtstream.WriteLine("}");
            txtstream.WriteLine("</style>");
            txtstream.WriteLine("</head>");
            txtstream.WriteLine("<body bgcolor='#333333'>");
            txtstream.WriteLine("<table colspacing='3' colpadding='3'>");
            txtstream.WriteLine("<tr>");
            for (var x = 0; x < Names.Count; x++)
            {
                txtstream.WriteLine("<th>" + Names(x) + "</th>");
            }
            txtstream.WriteLine("</tr>");
            txtstream.WriteLine("<xsl:for-each
select=\"data/Win32_Process\">");
            txtstream.WriteLine("<tr>");
            for (var x = 0; x < Names.Count; x++)
            {
                txtstream.WriteLine("<td><xsl:value-of
select=\"data/Win32_Process/" + Names(x) + "\"/></td>");
            }
            txtstream.WriteLine("</tr>");
            txtstream.WriteLine("</xsl:for-each>");
            txtstream.WriteLine("</table>");
```

```
            txtstream.WriteLine("</body>");
            txtstream.WriteLine("</html>");
            txtstream.WriteLine("</xsl:template>");
            txtstream.WriteLine("</xsl:stylesheet>");
            txtstream.Close();

            break;
        }
    case "Single Line Vertical":
        {
            txtstream.WriteLine("<?xml      version='1.0'      encoding='UTF-
8'?>");
            txtstream.WriteLine("<xsl:stylesheet                   version='1.0'
xmlns:xsl='http://www.w3.org/1999/XSL/Transform'>");
            txtstream.WriteLine("<xsl:template match=\"/\">");
            txtstream.WriteLine("<html>");
            txtstream.WriteLine("<head>");
            txtstream.WriteLine("<title>Products</title>");
            txtstream.WriteLine("<style type='text/css'>");
            txtstream.WriteLine("th");
            txtstream.WriteLine("{");
            txtstream.WriteLine("   COLOR: darkred;");
            txtstream.WriteLine("   BACKGROUND-COLOR: white;");
            txtstream.WriteLine("      FONT-FAMILY:font-family: Cambria,
serif;");
            txtstream.WriteLine("   FONT-SIZE: 12px;");
            txtstream.WriteLine("   text-align: left;");
            txtstream.WriteLine("   white-Space: nowrap;");
            txtstream.WriteLine("}");
            txtstream.WriteLine("td");
            txtstream.WriteLine("{");
            txtstream.WriteLine("   COLOR: navy;");
            txtstream.WriteLine("   BACKGROUND-COLOR: white;");
```

```
                    txtstream.WriteLine("      FONT-FAMILY: font-family: Cambria,
serif;");
                    txtstream.WriteLine("   FONT-SIZE: 12px;");
                    txtstream.WriteLine("   text-align: left;");
                    txtstream.WriteLine("   white-Space: nowrap;");
                    txtstream.WriteLine("}");
                    txtstream.WriteLine("</style>");
                    txtstream.WriteLine("</head>");
                    txtstream.WriteLine("<body bgcolor='#333333'>");
                    txtstream.WriteLine("<table colspacing='3' colpadding='3'>");
                    for (var x = 0; x < Names.Count; x++)
                    {
                        txtstream.WriteLine("<tr><th>" + Names(x) + "</th>");
                        txtstream.WriteLine("<td><xsl:value-of
select=\"data/Win32_Process/" + Names(x) + "\"/></td></tr>");
                    }
                    txtstream.WriteLine("</table>");
                    txtstream.WriteLine("</body>");
                    txtstream.WriteLine("</html>");
                    txtstream.WriteLine("</xsl:template>");
                    txtstream.WriteLine("</xsl:stylesheet>");
                    txtstream.Close();


                    break;

                }
            case "Multi Line Vertical":
                {

                    txtstream.WriteLine("<?xml     version='1.0'    encoding='UTF-
8'?>");
                    txtstream.WriteLine("<xsl:stylesheet              version='1.0'
xmlns:xsl='http://www.w3.org/1999/XSL/Transform'>");
```

```
txtstream.WriteLine("<xsl:template match=\"/\">");
txtstream.WriteLine("<html>");
txtstream.WriteLine("<head>");
txtstream.WriteLine("<title>Products</title>");
txtstream.WriteLine("<style type='text/css'>");
txtstream.WriteLine("th");
txtstream.WriteLine("{");
txtstream.WriteLine("   COLOR: darkred;");
txtstream.WriteLine("   BACKGROUND-COLOR: white;");
txtstream.WriteLine("      FONT-FAMILY:font-family: Cambria,
serif;");
txtstream.WriteLine("   FONT-SIZE: 12px;");
txtstream.WriteLine("   text-align: left;");
txtstream.WriteLine("   white-Space: nowrap;");
txtstream.WriteLine("}");
txtstream.WriteLine("td");
txtstream.WriteLine("{");
txtstream.WriteLine("   COLOR: navy;");
txtstream.WriteLine("   BACKGROUND-COLOR: white;");
txtstream.WriteLine("      FONT-FAMILY: font-family: Cambria,
serif;");
txtstream.WriteLine("   FONT-SIZE: 12px;");
txtstream.WriteLine("   text-align: left;");
txtstream.WriteLine("   white-Space: nowrap;");
txtstream.WriteLine("}");
txtstream.WriteLine("</style>");
txtstream.WriteLine("</head>");
txtstream.WriteLine("<body bgcolor='#333333'>");
txtstream.WriteLine("<table colspacing='3' colpadding='3'>");
for (var x = 0; x < Names.Count; x++)
{
    txtstream.WriteLine("<tr><th>" + Names(x) + "</th>");
```

```
                    txtstream.WriteLine("<td><xsl:for-each
select=\"data/Win32_Process\">");
                    txtstream.WriteLine("<xsl:value-of  select=\""  +  Names(x)  +
"\"/></td>");
                    txtstream.WriteLine("</xsl:for-each></tr>");
              }
              txtstream.WriteLine("</table>");
              txtstream.WriteLine("</body>");
              txtstream.WriteLine("</html>");
              txtstream.WriteLine("</xsl:template>");
              txtstream.WriteLine("</xsl:stylesheet>");
              txtstream.Close();
              break;
         }
     }
```

Stylesheets

The difference between boring and oh, wow!

The stylesheets in Appendix A, were used to render these pages. If you find one you like, feel free to use it.

Report:

Table

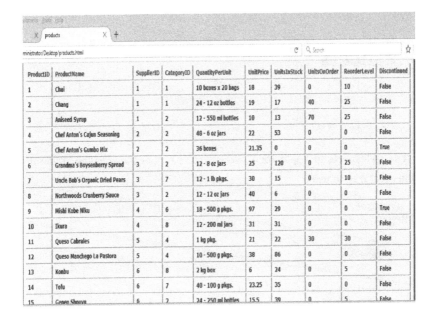

ProductID	ProductName	SupplierID	CategoryID	QuantityPerUnit	UnitPrice	UnitsInStock	UnitsOnOrder	ReorderLevel	Discontinued
1	Chai	1	1	10 boxes x 20 bags	18	39	0	10	False
2	Chang	1	1	24 - 12 oz bottles	19	17	40	25	False
3	Aniseed Syrup	1	2	12 - 550 ml bottles	10	13	70	25	False
4	Chef Anton's Cajun Seasoning	2	2	48 - 6 oz jars	22	53	0	0	False
5	Chef Anton's Gumbo Mix	2	2	36 boxes	21.35	0	0	0	True
6	Grandma's Boysenberry Spread	3	2	12 - 8 oz jars	25	120	0	25	False
7	Uncle Bob's Organic Dried Pears	3	7	12 - 1 lb pkgs.	30	15	0	10	False
8	Northwoods Cranberry Sauce	3	2	12 - 12 oz jars	40	6	0	0	False
9	Mishi Kobe Niku	4	6	18 - 500 g pkgs.	97	29	0	0	True
10	Ikura	4	8	12 - 200 ml jars	31	31	0	0	False
11	Queso Cabrales	5	4	1 kg pkg.	21	22	30	30	False
12	Queso Manchego La Pastora	5	4	10 - 500 g pkgs.	38	86	0	0	False
13	Konbu	6	8	2 kg box	6	24	0	5	False
14	Tofu	6	7	40 - 100 g pkgs.	23.25	35	0	0	False
15	Genen Shouyu	6	2	24 - 250 ml bottles	15.5	39	0	5	False

None:

Black and White

Colored:

AccountExpires	AuthorizationFlags	BadPasswordCount	Caption	CodePage	Comment	CountryCode	Description
			NT AUTHORITY\SYSTEM				Network login profile settings for SYSTEM on NT AUTHORITY
			NT AUTHORITY\LOCAL SERVICE				Network login profile settings for LOCAL SERVICE on NT AUTHORITY
			NT AUTHORITY\NETWORK SERVICE				Network login profile settings for NETWORK SERVICE on NT AUTHORITY
	0	0	Administrator	0	Built-in account for administering the computer/domain	0	Network login profile settings for on WIN-3JRLOAKMF5B
			NT SERVICE\%SASTELEMETRY				Network login profile settings for SSASTELEMETRY on NT SERVICE
			NT SERVICE\SSISTELEMETRY130				Network login profile settings for SSISTELEMETRY130 on NT SERVICE
			NT SERVICE\SQLTELEMETRY				Network login profile settings for SQLTELEMETRY on NT SERVICE
			NT SERVICE\MSSQLServerOLAPService				Network login profile settings for MSSQLServerOLAPService on NT SERVICE
			NT SERVICE\ReportServer				Network login profile settings for ReportServer on NT SERVICE
			NT SERVICE\MSSQLFDLauncher				Network login profile settings for MSSQLFDLauncher on NT SERVICE
			NT SERVICE\MSSQLLaunchpad				Network login profile settings for MSSQLLaunchpad on NT SERVICE
			NT SERVICE\MsDtsServer130				Network login profile settings for MsDtsServer130 on NT SERVICE
			NT SERVICE\MSSQLSERVER				Network login profile settings for MSSQLSERVER on NT SERVICE
			IIS APPPOOL\Classic .NET AppPool				Network login profile settings for Classic .NET AppPool on IIS APPPOOL
			IIS APPPOOL\.NET v4.5				Network login profile settings for .NET v4.5 on IIS APPPOOL
			IIS APPPOOL\.NET v2.0				Network login profile settings for .NET v2.0 on IIS APPPOOL
			IIS APPPOOL\.NET v4.5 Classic				Network login profile settings for .NET v4.5 Classic on IIS APPPOOL
			IIS APPPOOL\.NET v2.0 Classic				Network login profile settings for .NET v2.0 Classic on IIS APPPOOL

Oscillating:

Availability	BytesPerSector	Capabilities	CapabilityDescriptions	Caption	CompressionMethod	ConfigManagerErrorCode	ConfigManagerUserConfig
	512	3, 4, 10	Random Access, Supports Writing, SMART Notification	OCZ REVODRIVE350 SCSI Disk Device		0	FALSE
	512	3, 4	Random Access, Supports Writing	NVMe TOSHIBA-RD400		0	FALSE
	512	3, 4, 10	Random Access, Supports Writing, SMART Notification	TOSHIBA DT01ACA200		0	FALSE

3D:

Availability	BytesPerSector	Capabilities	CapabilityDescriptions	Caption	CompressionMethod	ConfigManagerErrorCode	ConfigManagerUserConfig	CreationClassName
	512	3, 4, 10	Random Access, Supports Writing, SMART Notification	OCZ REVODRIVE350 SCSI Disk Device		0	FALSE	Win32_DiskDrive
	512	3, 4	Random Access, Supports Writing	NVMe TOSHIBA-RD400		0	FALSE	Win32_DiskDrive
	512	3, 4, 10	Random Access, Supports Writing, SMART Notification	TOSHIBA DT01ACA200		0	FALSE	Win32_DiskDrive

Shadow Box:

Availability	BytesPerSector	Capabilities	CapabilityDescriptions	Caption	CompressionMethod	ConfigManagerErrorCode	ConfigManagerUserConfig	CreationClassName	DefaultBlockSize
	512	3, 4, 10	Random Access, Supports Writing, SMART Notification	OCZ REVODRIVE350 SCSI Disk Device		0	FALSE	Win32_DiskDrive	
	512	3, 4	Random Access, Supports Writing	NVMe TOSHIBA-RD400		0	FALSE	Win32_DiskDrive	
	512	3, 4, 10	Random Access, Supports Writing, SMART Notification	TOSHIBA DT01ACA200		0	FALSE	Win32_DiskDrive	

Shadow Box Single Line Vertical

BiosCharacteristics	7, 10, 11, 12, 15, 16, 17, 19, 23, 24, 25, 26, 27, 28, 29, 32, 33, 40, 42, 43, 48, 50, 58, 59, 64, 65, 66, 67, 68, 69, 70, 71, 72, 73, 74, 75, 76, 77, 78, 79
BIOSVersion	ALASKA - 1072009, 0504, American Megatrends - 5000C
BuildNumber	
Caption	0504
CodeSet	
CurrentLanguage	en|US|iso8859-1
Description	0504
IdentificationCode	
InstallableLanguages	8
InstallDate	
LanguageEdition	
ListOfLanguages	en|US|iso8859-1, fr|FR|iso8859-1, zh|CN|unicode, , , , ,
Manufacturer	American Megatrends Inc.
Name	0504
OtherTargetOS	
PrimaryBIOS	TRUE

Shadow Box Multi line Vertical

Availability			
BytesPerSector	512	512	512
Capabilities	3, 4, 10	3, 4	3, 4, 10
CapabilityDescriptions	Random Access, Supports Writing, SMART Notification	Random Access, Supports Writing	Random Access, Supports Writing, SMART Notification
Caption	OCZ REVODRIVE350 SCSI Disk Device	NVMe TOSHIBA-RG400	TOSHIBA DT01ACA300
CompressionMethod			
ConfigManagerErrorCode	0	0	0
ConfigManagerUserConfig	FALSE	FALSE	FALSE
CreationClassName	Win32_DiskDrive	Win32_DiskDrive	Win32_DiskDrive
DefaultBlockSize			
Description	Disk drive	Disk drive	Disk drive
DeviceID	\\.\PHYSICALDRIVE2	\\.\PHYSICALDRIVE1	\\.\PHYSICALDRIVE0
ErrorCleared			
ErrorDescription			
ErrorMethodology			
FirmwareRevision	1.09	FNCX4101	MX4OABB0
Index	2	1	0

STYLESHEETS CODE

Decorating your web pages

BELOW ARE SOME STYLESHEETS I COOKED UP THAT I LIKE AND THINK YOU MIGHT TOO. Don't worry I won't be offended if you take and modify to your hearts delight. Please do!

NONE

```
txtstream.WriteLine("<style type='text/css'>“);
txtstream.WriteLine("th”);
txtstream.WriteLine("{“);
txtstream.WriteLine("    COLOR: darkred;”);
txtstream.WriteLine("}”);
txtstream.WriteLine("td”);
txtstream.WriteLine("{“);
txtstream.WriteLine("    COLOR: Navy;”);
txtstream.WriteLine("}”);
txtstream.WriteLine("</style>“);
```

BLACK AND WHITE TEXT

```
txtstream.WriteLine("<style type='text/css'>“);
txtstream.WriteLine("th”);
```

```
txtstream.WriteLine("{");
txtstream.WriteLine("    COLOR: white;");
txtstream.WriteLine("    BACKGROUND-COLOR: black;");
txtstream.WriteLine("    FONT-FAMILY:font-family: Cambria, serif;");
txtstream.WriteLine("    FONT-SIZE: 12px;");
txtstream.WriteLine("    text-align: left;");
txtstream.WriteLine("    white-Space: nowrap;");
txtstream.WriteLine("}");
txtstream.WriteLine("td");
txtstream.WriteLine("{");
txtstream.WriteLine("    COLOR: white;");
txtstream.WriteLine("    BACKGROUND-COLOR: black;");
txtstream.WriteLine("    FONT-FAMILY: font-family: Cambria, serif;");
txtstream.WriteLine("    FONT-SIZE: 12px;");
txtstream.WriteLine("    text-align: left;");
txtstream.WriteLine("    white-Space: nowrap;");
txtstream.WriteLine("}");
txtstream.WriteLine("div");
txtstream.WriteLine("{");
txtstream.WriteLine("    COLOR: white;");
txtstream.WriteLine("    BACKGROUND-COLOR: black;");
txtstream.WriteLine("    FONT-FAMILY: font-family: Cambria, serif;");
txtstream.WriteLine("    FONT-SIZE: 10px;");
txtstream.WriteLine("    text-align: left;");
txtstream.WriteLine("    white-Space: nowrap;");
txtstream.WriteLine("}");
txtstream.WriteLine("span");
txtstream.WriteLine("{");
txtstream.WriteLine("    COLOR: white;");
txtstream.WriteLine("    BACKGROUND-COLOR: black;");
txtstream.WriteLine("    FONT-FAMILY: font-family: Cambria, serif;");
txtstream.WriteLine("    FONT-SIZE: 10px;");
txtstream.WriteLine("    text-align: left;");
```

```
txtstream.WriteLine("   white-Space: nowrap;");
txtstream.WriteLine("   display:inline-block;");
txtstream.WriteLine("   width: 100%;");
txtstream.WriteLine("}");
txtstream.WriteLine("textarea");
txtstream.WriteLine("{");
txtstream.WriteLine("   COLOR: white;");
txtstream.WriteLine("   BACKGROUND-COLOR: black;");
txtstream.WriteLine("   FONT-FAMILY: font-family: Cambria, serif;");
txtstream.WriteLine("   FONT-SIZE: 10px;");
txtstream.WriteLine("   text-align: left;");
txtstream.WriteLine("   white-Space: nowrap;");
txtstream.WriteLine("   width: 100%;");
txtstream.WriteLine("}");
txtstream.WriteLine("select");
txtstream.WriteLine("{");
txtstream.WriteLine("   COLOR: white;");
txtstream.WriteLine("   BACKGROUND-COLOR: black;");
txtstream.WriteLine("   FONT-FAMILY: font-family: Cambria, serif;");
txtstream.WriteLine("   FONT-SIZE: 10px;");
txtstream.WriteLine("   text-align: left;");
txtstream.WriteLine("   white-Space: nowrap;");
txtstream.WriteLine("   width: 100%;");
txtstream.WriteLine("}");
txtstream.WriteLine("input");
txtstream.WriteLine("{");
txtstream.WriteLine("   COLOR: white;");
txtstream.WriteLine("   BACKGROUND-COLOR: black;");
txtstream.WriteLine("   FONT-FAMILY: font-family: Cambria, serif;");
txtstream.WriteLine("   FONT-SIZE: 12px;");
txtstream.WriteLine("   text-align: left;");
txtstream.WriteLine("   display:table-cell;");
txtstream.WriteLine("   white-Space: nowrap;");
```

```
txtstream.WriteLine("}");
txtstream.WriteLine("h1 {");
txtstream.WriteLine("color: antiquewhite;");
txtstream.WriteLine("text-shadow: 1px 1px 1px black;");
txtstream.WriteLine("padding: 3px;");
txtstream.WriteLine("text-align: center;");
txtstream.WriteLine("box-shadow: inset 2px 2px 5px rgba(0,0,0,0.5), inset -
2px -2px 5px rgba(255,255,255,0.5)");
txtstream.WriteLine("}");
txtstream.WriteLine("</style>");
```

COLORED TEXT

```
txtstream.WriteLine("<style type='text/css'>");
txtstream.WriteLine("th");
txtstream.WriteLine("{");
txtstream.WriteLine("   COLOR: darkred;");
txtstream.WriteLine("   BACKGROUND-COLOR: #eeeeee;");
txtstream.WriteLine("   FONT-FAMILY:font-family: Cambria, serif;");
txtstream.WriteLine("   FONT-SIZE: 12px;");
txtstream.WriteLine("   text-align: left;");
txtstream.WriteLine("   white-Space: nowrap;");
txtstream.WriteLine("}");
txtstream.WriteLine("td");
txtstream.WriteLine("{");
txtstream.WriteLine("   COLOR: navy;");
txtstream.WriteLine("   BACKGROUND-COLOR: #eeeeee;");
txtstream.WriteLine("   FONT-FAMILY: font-family: Cambria, serif;");
txtstream.WriteLine("   FONT-SIZE: 12px;");
txtstream.WriteLine("   text-align: left;");
txtstream.WriteLine("   white-Space: nowrap;");
txtstream.WriteLine("}");
txtstream.WriteLine("div");
```

```
txtstream.WriteLine("{");
txtstream.WriteLine("    COLOR: white;");
txtstream.WriteLine("    BACKGROUND-COLOR: navy;");
txtstream.WriteLine("    FONT-FAMILY: font-family: Cambria, serif;");
txtstream.WriteLine("    FONT-SIZE: 10px;");
txtstream.WriteLine("    text-align: left;");
txtstream.WriteLine("    white-Space: nowrap;");
txtstream.WriteLine("}");
txtstream.WriteLine("span");
txtstream.WriteLine("{");
txtstream.WriteLine("    COLOR: white;");
txtstream.WriteLine("    BACKGROUND-COLOR: navy;");
txtstream.WriteLine("    FONT-FAMILY: font-family: Cambria, serif;");
txtstream.WriteLine("    FONT-SIZE: 10px;");
txtstream.WriteLine("    text-align: left;");
txtstream.WriteLine("    white-Space: nowrap;");
txtstream.WriteLine("    display:inline-block;");
txtstream.WriteLine("    width: 100%;");
txtstream.WriteLine("}");
txtstream.WriteLine("textarea");
txtstream.WriteLine("{");
txtstream.WriteLine("    COLOR: white;");
txtstream.WriteLine("    BACKGROUND-COLOR: navy;");
txtstream.WriteLine("    FONT-FAMILY: font-family: Cambria, serif;");
txtstream.WriteLine("    FONT-SIZE: 10px;");
txtstream.WriteLine("    text-align: left;");
txtstream.WriteLine("    white-Space: nowrap;");
txtstream.WriteLine("    width: 100%;");
txtstream.WriteLine("}");
txtstream.WriteLine("select");
txtstream.WriteLine("{");
txtstream.WriteLine("    COLOR: white;");
txtstream.WriteLine("    BACKGROUND-COLOR: navy;");
```

txtstream.WriteLine("   FONT-FAMILY: font-family: Cambria, serif;");
txtstream.WriteLine("   FONT-SIZE: 10px;");
txtstream.WriteLine("   text-align: left;");
txtstream.WriteLine("   white-Space: nowrap;");
txtstream.WriteLine("   width: 100%;");
txtstream.WriteLine("}");
txtstream.WriteLine("input");
txtstream.WriteLine("{“);
txtstream.WriteLine("   COLOR: white;");
txtstream.WriteLine("   BACKGROUND-COLOR: navy;");
txtstream.WriteLine("   FONT-FAMILY: font-family: Cambria, serif;");
txtstream.WriteLine("   FONT-SIZE: 12px;");
txtstream.WriteLine("   text-align: left;");
txtstream.WriteLine("   display:table-cell;");
txtstream.WriteLine("   white-Space: nowrap;");
txtstream.WriteLine("}");
txtstream.WriteLine("h1 {“);
txtstream.WriteLine("color: antiquewhite;");
txtstream.WriteLine("text-shadow: 1px 1px 1px black;");
txtstream.WriteLine("padding: 3px;");
txtstream.WriteLine("text-align: center;");
txtstream.WriteLine("box-shadow: inset 2px 2px 5px rgba(0,0,0,0.5), inset -2px -2px 5px rgba(255,255,255,0.5)");
txtstream.WriteLine("}");
txtstream.WriteLine("</style>“);

OSCILLATING ROW COLORS

txtstream.WriteLine("<style>“);
txtstream.WriteLine("th");
txtstream.WriteLine("{“);

```
txtstream.WriteLine("    COLOR: white;");
txtstream.WriteLine("    BACKGROUND-COLOR: navy;");
txtstream.WriteLine("    FONT-FAMILY:font-family: Cambria, serif;");
txtstream.WriteLine("    FONT-SIZE: 12px;");
txtstream.WriteLine("    text-align: left;");
txtstream.WriteLine("    white-Space: nowrap;");
txtstream.WriteLine("}");
txtstream.WriteLine("td");
txtstream.WriteLine("{");
txtstream.WriteLine("    COLOR: navy;");
txtstream.WriteLine("    FONT-FAMILY: font-family: Cambria, serif;");
txtstream.WriteLine("    FONT-SIZE: 12px;");
txtstream.WriteLine("    text-align: left;");
txtstream.WriteLine("    white-Space: nowrap;");
txtstream.WriteLine("}");
txtstream.WriteLine("div");
txtstream.WriteLine("{");
txtstream.WriteLine("    COLOR: navy;");
txtstream.WriteLine("    FONT-FAMILY: font-family: Cambria, serif;");
txtstream.WriteLine("    FONT-SIZE: 12px;");
txtstream.WriteLine("    text-align: left;");
txtstream.WriteLine("    white-Space: nowrap;");
txtstream.WriteLine("}");
txtstream.WriteLine("span");
txtstream.WriteLine("{");
txtstream.WriteLine("    COLOR: navy;");
txtstream.WriteLine("    FONT-FAMILY: font-family: Cambria, serif;");
txtstream.WriteLine("    FONT-SIZE: 12px;");
txtstream.WriteLine("    text-align: left;");
txtstream.WriteLine("    white-Space: nowrap;");
txtstream.WriteLine("    width: 100%;");
txtstream.WriteLine("}");
txtstream.WriteLine("textarea");
```

```
txtstream.WriteLine("{“);
txtstream.WriteLine("   COLOR: navy;”);
txtstream.WriteLine("   FONT-FAMILY: font-family: Cambria, serif;”);
txtstream.WriteLine("   FONT-SIZE: 12px;”);
txtstream.WriteLine("   text-align: left;”);
txtstream.WriteLine("   white-Space: nowrap;”);
txtstream.WriteLine("   display:inline-block;”);
txtstream.WriteLine("   width: 100%;”);
txtstream.WriteLine("}”);
txtstream.WriteLine("select”);
txtstream.WriteLine("{“);
txtstream.WriteLine("   COLOR: navy;”);
txtstream.WriteLine("   FONT-FAMILY: font-family: Cambria, serif;”);
txtstream.WriteLine("   FONT-SIZE: 10px;”);
txtstream.WriteLine("   text-align: left;”);
txtstream.WriteLine("   white-Space: nowrap;”);
txtstream.WriteLine("   display:inline-block;”);
txtstream.WriteLine("   width: 100%;”);
txtstream.WriteLine("}”);
txtstream.WriteLine("input”);
txtstream.WriteLine("{“);
txtstream.WriteLine("   COLOR: navy;”);
txtstream.WriteLine("   FONT-FAMILY: font-family: Cambria, serif;”);
txtstream.WriteLine("   FONT-SIZE: 12px;”);
txtstream.WriteLine("   text-align: left;”);
txtstream.WriteLine("   display:table-cell;”);
txtstream.WriteLine("   white-Space: nowrap;”);
txtstream.WriteLine("}”);
txtstream.WriteLine("h1 {“);
txtstream.WriteLine("color: antiquewhite;”);
txtstream.WriteLine("text-shadow: 1px 1px 1px black;”);
txtstream.WriteLine("padding: 3px;”);
txtstream.WriteLine("text-align: center;”);
```

txtstream.WriteLine("box-shadow: inset 2px 2px 5px rgba(0,0,0,0.5), inset -2px -2px 5px rgba(255,255,255,0.5)");

txtstream.WriteLine("}");

txtstream.WriteLine("tr:nth-child(even){background-color:#f2f2f2;}");

txtstream.WriteLine("tr:nth-child(odd){background-color:#cccccc; color:#f2f2f2;}");

txtstream.WriteLine("</style>");

GHOST DECORATED

txtstream.WriteLine("<style type='text/css'>");

txtstream.WriteLine("th");

txtstream.WriteLine("{");

txtstream.WriteLine("   COLOR: black;");

txtstream.WriteLine("   BACKGROUND-COLOR: white;");

txtstream.WriteLine("   FONT-FAMILY:font-family: Cambria, serif;");

txtstream.WriteLine("   FONT-SIZE: 12px;");

txtstream.WriteLine("   text-align: left;");

txtstream.WriteLine("   white-Space: nowrap;");

txtstream.WriteLine("}");

txtstream.WriteLine("td");

txtstream.WriteLine("{");

txtstream.WriteLine("   COLOR: black;");

txtstream.WriteLine("   BACKGROUND-COLOR: white;");

txtstream.WriteLine("   FONT-FAMILY: font-family: Cambria, serif;");

txtstream.WriteLine("   FONT-SIZE: 12px;");

txtstream.WriteLine("   text-align: left;");

txtstream.WriteLine("   white-Space: nowrap;");

txtstream.WriteLine("}");

txtstream.WriteLine("div");

txtstream.WriteLine("{");

txtstream.WriteLine("   COLOR: black;");

txtstream.WriteLine("   BACKGROUND-COLOR: white;");

```
txtstream.WriteLine("    FONT-FAMILY: font-family: Cambria, serif;");
txtstream.WriteLine("    FONT-SIZE: 10px;");
txtstream.WriteLine("    text-align: left;");
txtstream.WriteLine("    white-Space: nowrap;");
txtstream.WriteLine("}");
txtstream.WriteLine("span");
txtstream.WriteLine("{");
txtstream.WriteLine("    COLOR: black;");
txtstream.WriteLine("    BACKGROUND-COLOR: white;");
txtstream.WriteLine("    FONT-FAMILY: font-family: Cambria, serif;");
txtstream.WriteLine("    FONT-SIZE: 10px;");
txtstream.WriteLine("    text-align: left;");
txtstream.WriteLine("    white-Space: nowrap;");
txtstream.WriteLine("    display:inline-block;");
txtstream.WriteLine("    width: 100%;");
txtstream.WriteLine("}");
txtstream.WriteLine("textarea");
txtstream.WriteLine("{");
txtstream.WriteLine("    COLOR: black;");
txtstream.WriteLine("    BACKGROUND-COLOR: white;");
txtstream.WriteLine("    FONT-FAMILY: font-family: Cambria, serif;");
txtstream.WriteLine("    FONT-SIZE: 10px;");
txtstream.WriteLine("    text-align: left;");
txtstream.WriteLine("    white-Space: nowrap;");
txtstream.WriteLine("    width: 100%;");
txtstream.WriteLine("}");
txtstream.WriteLine("select");
txtstream.WriteLine("{");
txtstream.WriteLine("    COLOR: black;");
txtstream.WriteLine("    BACKGROUND-COLOR: white;");
txtstream.WriteLine("    FONT-FAMILY: font-family: Cambria, serif;");
txtstream.WriteLine("    FONT-SIZE: 10px;");
txtstream.WriteLine("    text-align: left;");
```

```
txtstream.WriteLine("   white-Space: nowrap;");
txtstream.WriteLine("   width: 100%;");
txtstream.WriteLine("}");
txtstream.WriteLine("input");
txtstream.WriteLine("{");
txtstream.WriteLine("   COLOR: black;");
txtstream.WriteLine("   BACKGROUND-COLOR: white;");
txtstream.WriteLine("   FONT-FAMILY: font-family: Cambria, serif;");
txtstream.WriteLine("   FONT-SIZE: 12px;");
txtstream.WriteLine("   text-align: left;");
txtstream.WriteLine("   display:table-cell;");
txtstream.WriteLine("   white-Space: nowrap;");
txtstream.WriteLine("}");
txtstream.WriteLine("h1 {");
txtstream.WriteLine("color: antiquewhite;");
txtstream.WriteLine("text-shadow: 1px 1px 1px black;");
txtstream.WriteLine("padding: 3px;");
txtstream.WriteLine("text-align: center;");
txtstream.WriteLine("box-shadow: inset 2px 2px 5px rgba(0,0,0,0.5), inset -
2px -2px 5px rgba(255,255,255,0.5)");
txtstream.WriteLine("}");
txtstream.WriteLine("</style>");
```

3D

```
txtstream.WriteLine("<style type='text/css'>");
txtstream.WriteLine("body");
txtstream.WriteLine("{");
txtstream.WriteLine("   PADDING-RIGHT: 0px;");
txtstream.WriteLine("   PADDING-LEFT: 0px;");
txtstream.WriteLine("   PADDING-BOTTOM: 0px;");
txtstream.WriteLine("   MARGIN: 0px;");
```

```
txtstream.WriteLine("    COLOR: #333;");
txtstream.WriteLine("    PADDING-TOP: 0px;");
txtstream.WriteLine("    FONT-FAMILY: verdana, arial, helvetica, sans-serif;");
txtstream.WriteLine("}");
txtstream.WriteLine("table");
txtstream.WriteLine("{");
txtstream.WriteLine("    BORDER-RIGHT: #999999 3px solid;");
txtstream.WriteLine("    PADDING-RIGHT: 6px;");
txtstream.WriteLine("    PADDING-LEFT: 6px;");
txtstream.WriteLine("    FONT-WEIGHT: Bold;");
txtstream.WriteLine("    FONT-SIZE: 14px;");
txtstream.WriteLine("    PADDING-BOTTOM: 6px;");
txtstream.WriteLine("    COLOR: Peru;");
txtstream.WriteLine("    LINE-HEIGHT: 14px;");
txtstream.WriteLine("    PADDING-TOP: 6px;");
txtstream.WriteLine("    BORDER-BOTTOM: #999 1px solid;");
txtstream.WriteLine("    BACKGROUND-COLOR: #eeeeee;");
txtstream.WriteLine("    FONT-FAMILY: verdana, arial, helvetica, sans-serif;");
txtstream.WriteLine("    FONT-SIZE: 12px;");
txtstream.WriteLine("}");
txtstream.WriteLine("th");
txtstream.WriteLine("{");
txtstream.WriteLine("    BORDER-RIGHT: #999999 3px solid;");
txtstream.WriteLine("    PADDING-RIGHT: 6px;");
txtstream.WriteLine("    PADDING-LEFT: 6px;");
txtstream.WriteLine("    FONT-WEIGHT: Bold;");
txtstream.WriteLine("    FONT-SIZE: 14px;");
txtstream.WriteLine("    PADDING-BOTTOM: 6px;");
txtstream.WriteLine("    COLOR: darkred;");
txtstream.WriteLine("    LINE-HEIGHT: 14px;");
txtstream.WriteLine("    PADDING-TOP: 6px;");
txtstream.WriteLine("    BORDER-BOTTOM: #999 1px solid;");
txtstream.WriteLine("    BACKGROUND-COLOR: #eeeeee;");
```

```
txtstream.WriteLine("   FONT-FAMILY:font-family: Cambria, serif;");
txtstream.WriteLine("   FONT-SIZE: 12px;");
txtstream.WriteLine("   text-align: left;");
txtstream.WriteLine("   white-Space: nowrap;");
txtstream.WriteLine("}");
txtstream.WriteLine(".th");
txtstream.WriteLine("{");
txtstream.WriteLine("   BORDER-RIGHT: #999999 2px solid;");
txtstream.WriteLine("   PADDING-RIGHT: 6px;");
txtstream.WriteLine("   PADDING-LEFT: 6px;");
txtstream.WriteLine("   FONT-WEIGHT: Bold;");
txtstream.WriteLine("   PADDING-BOTTOM: 6px;");
txtstream.WriteLine("   COLOR: black;");
txtstream.WriteLine("   PADDING-TOP: 6px;");
txtstream.WriteLine("   BORDER-BOTTOM: #999 2px solid;");
txtstream.WriteLine("   BACKGROUND-COLOR: #eeeeee;");
txtstream.WriteLine("   FONT-FAMILY: font-family: Cambria, serif;");
txtstream.WriteLine("   FONT-SIZE: 10px;");
txtstream.WriteLine("   text-align: right;");
txtstream.WriteLine("   white-Space: nowrap;");
txtstream.WriteLine("}");
txtstream.WriteLine("td");
txtstream.WriteLine("{");
txtstream.WriteLine("   BORDER-RIGHT: #999999 3px solid;");
txtstream.WriteLine("   PADDING-RIGHT: 6px;");
txtstream.WriteLine("   PADDING-LEFT: 6px;");
txtstream.WriteLine("   FONT-WEIGHT: Normal;");
txtstream.WriteLine("   PADDING-BOTTOM: 6px;");
txtstream.WriteLine("   COLOR: navy;");
txtstream.WriteLine("   LINE-HEIGHT: 14px;");
txtstream.WriteLine("   PADDING-TOP: 6px;");
txtstream.WriteLine("   BORDER-BOTTOM: #999 1px solid;");
txtstream.WriteLine("   BACKGROUND-COLOR: #eeeeee;");
```

```
txtstream.WriteLine("   FONT-FAMILY: font-family: Cambria, serif;");
txtstream.WriteLine("   FONT-SIZE: 12px;");
txtstream.WriteLine("   text-align: left;");
txtstream.WriteLine("   white-Space: nowrap;");
txtstream.WriteLine("}");
txtstream.WriteLine("div");
txtstream.WriteLine("{");
txtstream.WriteLine("   BORDER-RIGHT: #999999 3px solid;");
txtstream.WriteLine("   PADDING-RIGHT: 6px;");
txtstream.WriteLine("   PADDING-LEFT: 6px;");
txtstream.WriteLine("   FONT-WEIGHT: Normal;");
txtstream.WriteLine("   PADDING-BOTTOM: 6px;");
txtstream.WriteLine("   COLOR: white;");
txtstream.WriteLine("   PADDING-TOP: 6px;");
txtstream.WriteLine("   BORDER-BOTTOM: #999 1px solid;");
txtstream.WriteLine("   BACKGROUND-COLOR: navy;");
txtstream.WriteLine("   FONT-FAMILY: font-family: Cambria, serif;");
txtstream.WriteLine("   FONT-SIZE: 10px;");
txtstream.WriteLine("   text-align: left;");
txtstream.WriteLine("   white-Space: nowrap;");
txtstream.WriteLine("}");
txtstream.WriteLine("span");
txtstream.WriteLine("{");
txtstream.WriteLine("   BORDER-RIGHT: #999999 3px solid;");
txtstream.WriteLine("   PADDING-RIGHT: 3px;");
txtstream.WriteLine("   PADDING-LEFT: 3px;");
txtstream.WriteLine("   FONT-WEIGHT: Normal;");
txtstream.WriteLine("   PADDING-BOTTOM: 3px;");
txtstream.WriteLine("   COLOR: white;");
txtstream.WriteLine("   PADDING-TOP: 3px;");
txtstream.WriteLine("   BORDER-BOTTOM: #999 1px solid;");
txtstream.WriteLine("   BACKGROUND-COLOR: navy;");
txtstream.WriteLine("   FONT-FAMILY: font-family: Cambria, serif;");
```

```
txtstream.WriteLine("    FONT-SIZE: 10px;");
txtstream.WriteLine("    text-align: left;");
txtstream.WriteLine("    white-Space: nowrap;");
txtstream.WriteLine("    display:inline-block;");
txtstream.WriteLine("    width: 100%;");
txtstream.WriteLine("}");
txtstream.WriteLine("textarea");
txtstream.WriteLine("{");
txtstream.WriteLine("    BORDER-RIGHT: #999999 3px solid;");
txtstream.WriteLine("    PADDING-RIGHT: 3px;");
txtstream.WriteLine("    PADDING-LEFT: 3px;");
txtstream.WriteLine("    FONT-WEIGHT: Normal;");
txtstream.WriteLine("    PADDING-BOTTOM: 3px;");
txtstream.WriteLine("    COLOR: white;");
txtstream.WriteLine("    PADDING-TOP: 3px;");
txtstream.WriteLine("    BORDER-BOTTOM: #999 1px solid;");
txtstream.WriteLine("    BACKGROUND-COLOR: navy;");
txtstream.WriteLine("    FONT-FAMILY: font-family: Cambria, serif;");
txtstream.WriteLine("    FONT-SIZE: 10px;");
txtstream.WriteLine("    text-align: left;");
txtstream.WriteLine("    white-Space: nowrap;");
txtstream.WriteLine("    width: 100%;");
txtstream.WriteLine("}");
txtstream.WriteLine("select");
txtstream.WriteLine("{");
txtstream.WriteLine("    BORDER-RIGHT: #999999 3px solid;");
txtstream.WriteLine("    PADDING-RIGHT: 6px;");
txtstream.WriteLine("    PADDING-LEFT: 6px;");
txtstream.WriteLine("    FONT-WEIGHT: Normal;");
txtstream.WriteLine("    PADDING-BOTTOM: 6px;");
txtstream.WriteLine("    COLOR: white;");
txtstream.WriteLine("    PADDING-TOP: 6px;");
txtstream.WriteLine("    BORDER-BOTTOM: #999 1px solid;");
```

```
txtstream.WriteLine("    BACKGROUND-COLOR: navy;");
txtstream.WriteLine("    FONT-FAMILY: font-family: Cambria, serif;");
txtstream.WriteLine("    FONT-SIZE: 10px;");
txtstream.WriteLine("    text-align: left;");
txtstream.WriteLine("    white-Space: nowrap;");
txtstream.WriteLine("    width: 100%;");
txtstream.WriteLine("}");
txtstream.WriteLine("input");
txtstream.WriteLine("{");
txtstream.WriteLine("    BORDER-RIGHT: #999999 3px solid;");
txtstream.WriteLine("    PADDING-RIGHT: 3px;");
txtstream.WriteLine("    PADDING-LEFT: 3px;");
txtstream.WriteLine("    FONT-WEIGHT: Bold;");
txtstream.WriteLine("    PADDING-BOTTOM: 3px;");
txtstream.WriteLine("    COLOR: white;");
txtstream.WriteLine("    PADDING-TOP: 3px;");
txtstream.WriteLine("    BORDER-BOTTOM: #999 1px solid;");
txtstream.WriteLine("    BACKGROUND-COLOR: navy;");
txtstream.WriteLine("    FONT-FAMILY: font-family: Cambria, serif;");
txtstream.WriteLine("    FONT-SIZE: 12px;");
txtstream.WriteLine("    text-align: left;");
txtstream.WriteLine("    display:table-cell;");
txtstream.WriteLine("    white-Space: nowrap;");
txtstream.WriteLine("    width: 100%;");
txtstream.WriteLine("}");
txtstream.WriteLine("h1 {");
txtstream.WriteLine("color: antiquewhite;");
txtstream.WriteLine("text-shadow: 1px 1px 1px black;");
txtstream.WriteLine("padding: 3px;");
txtstream.WriteLine("text-align: center;");
txtstream.WriteLine("box-shadow: inset 2px 2px 5px rgba(0,0,0,0.5), inset -2px -2px 5px rgba(255,255,255,0.5)");
txtstream.WriteLine("}");
```

txtstream.WriteLine("</style>");

SHADOW BOX

txtstream.WriteLine("<style type='text/css'>");
txtstream.WriteLine("body");
txtstream.WriteLine("{");
txtstream.WriteLine("   PADDING-RIGHT: 0px;");
txtstream.WriteLine("   PADDING-LEFT: 0px;");
txtstream.WriteLine("   PADDING-BOTTOM: 0px;");
txtstream.WriteLine("   MARGIN: 0px;");
txtstream.WriteLine("   COLOR: #333;");
txtstream.WriteLine("   PADDING-TOP: 0px;");
txtstream.WriteLine("   FONT-FAMILY: verdana, arial, helvetica, sans-serif;");
txtstream.WriteLine("}");
txtstream.WriteLine("table");
txtstream.WriteLine("{");
txtstream.WriteLine("   BORDER-RIGHT: #999999 1px solid;");
txtstream.WriteLine("   PADDING-RIGHT: 1px;");
txtstream.WriteLine("   PADDING-LEFT: 1px;");
txtstream.WriteLine("   PADDING-BOTTOM: 1px;");
txtstream.WriteLine("   LINE-HEIGHT: 8px;");
txtstream.WriteLine("   PADDING-TOP: 1px;");
txtstream.WriteLine("   BORDER-BOTTOM: #999 1px solid;");
txtstream.WriteLine("   BACKGROUND-COLOR: #eeeeee;");
txtstream.WriteLine("   filter:progid:DXImageTransform.Microsoft.Shadow(color='silver',   Direction=135, Strength=16)");
txtstream.WriteLine("}");
txtstream.WriteLine("th");
txtstream.WriteLine("{");
txtstream.WriteLine("   BORDER-RIGHT: #999999 3px solid;");
txtstream.WriteLine("   PADDING-RIGHT: 6px;");

```
txtstream.WriteLine("    PADDING-LEFT: 6px;");
txtstream.WriteLine("    FONT-WEIGHT: Bold;");
txtstream.WriteLine("    FONT-SIZE: 14px;");
txtstream.WriteLine("    PADDING-BOTTOM: 6px;");
txtstream.WriteLine("    COLOR: darkred;");
txtstream.WriteLine("    LINE-HEIGHT: 14px;");
txtstream.WriteLine("    PADDING-TOP: 6px;");
txtstream.WriteLine("    BORDER-BOTTOM: #999 1px solid;");
txtstream.WriteLine("    BACKGROUND-COLOR: #eeeeee;");
txtstream.WriteLine("    FONT-FAMILY: font-family: Cambria, serif;");
txtstream.WriteLine("    FONT-SIZE: 12px;");
txtstream.WriteLine("    text-align: left;");
txtstream.WriteLine("    white-Space: nowrap;");
txtstream.WriteLine("}");
txtstream.WriteLine(".th");
txtstream.WriteLine("{");
txtstream.WriteLine("    BORDER-RIGHT: #999999 2px solid;");
txtstream.WriteLine("    PADDING-RIGHT: 6px;");
txtstream.WriteLine("    PADDING-LEFT: 6px;");
txtstream.WriteLine("    FONT-WEIGHT: Bold;");
txtstream.WriteLine("    PADDING-BOTTOM: 6px;");
txtstream.WriteLine("    COLOR: black;");
txtstream.WriteLine("    PADDING-TOP: 6px;");
txtstream.WriteLine("    BORDER-BOTTOM: #999 2px solid;");
txtstream.WriteLine("    BACKGROUND-COLOR: #eeeeee;");
txtstream.WriteLine("    FONT-FAMILY: font-family: Cambria, serif;");
txtstream.WriteLine("    FONT-SIZE: 10px;");
txtstream.WriteLine("    text-align: right;");
txtstream.WriteLine("    white-Space: nowrap;");
txtstream.WriteLine("}");
txtstream.WriteLine("td");
txtstream.WriteLine("{");
txtstream.WriteLine("    BORDER-RIGHT: #999999 3px solid;");
```

```
txtstream.WriteLine("    PADDING-RIGHT: 6px;");
txtstream.WriteLine("    PADDING-LEFT: 6px;");
txtstream.WriteLine("    FONT-WEIGHT: Normal;");
txtstream.WriteLine("    PADDING-BOTTOM: 6px;");
txtstream.WriteLine("    COLOR: navy;");
txtstream.WriteLine("    LINE-HEIGHT: 14px;");
txtstream.WriteLine("    PADDING-TOP: 6px;");
txtstream.WriteLine("    BORDER-BOTTOM: #999 1px solid;");
txtstream.WriteLine("    BACKGROUND-COLOR: #eeeeee;");
txtstream.WriteLine("    FONT-FAMILY: font-family: Cambria, serif;");
txtstream.WriteLine("    FONT-SIZE: 12px;");
txtstream.WriteLine("    text-align: left;");
txtstream.WriteLine("    white-Space: nowrap;");
txtstream.WriteLine("}");
txtstream.WriteLine("div");
txtstream.WriteLine("{");
txtstream.WriteLine("    BORDER-RIGHT: #999999 3px solid;");
txtstream.WriteLine("    PADDING-RIGHT: 6px;");
txtstream.WriteLine("    PADDING-LEFT: 6px;");
txtstream.WriteLine("    FONT-WEIGHT: Normal;");
txtstream.WriteLine("    PADDING-BOTTOM: 6px;");
txtstream.WriteLine("    COLOR: white;");
txtstream.WriteLine("    PADDING-TOP: 6px;");
txtstream.WriteLine("    BORDER-BOTTOM: #999 1px solid;");
txtstream.WriteLine("    BACKGROUND-COLOR: navy;");
txtstream.WriteLine("    FONT-FAMILY: font-family: Cambria, serif;");
txtstream.WriteLine("    FONT-SIZE: 10px;");
txtstream.WriteLine("    text-align: left;");
txtstream.WriteLine("    white-Space: nowrap;");
txtstream.WriteLine("}");
txtstream.WriteLine("span");
txtstream.WriteLine("{");
txtstream.WriteLine("    BORDER-RIGHT: #999999 3px solid;");
```

```
txtstream.WriteLine("   PADDING-RIGHT: 3px;");
txtstream.WriteLine("   PADDING-LEFT: 3px;");
txtstream.WriteLine("   FONT-WEIGHT: Normal;");
txtstream.WriteLine("   PADDING-BOTTOM: 3px;");
txtstream.WriteLine("   COLOR: white;");
txtstream.WriteLine("   PADDING-TOP: 3px;");
txtstream.WriteLine("   BORDER-BOTTOM: #999 1px solid;");
txtstream.WriteLine("   BACKGROUND-COLOR: navy;");
txtstream.WriteLine("   FONT-FAMILY: font-family: Cambria, serif;");
txtstream.WriteLine("   FONT-SIZE: 10px;");
txtstream.WriteLine("   text-align: left;");
txtstream.WriteLine("   white-Space: nowrap;");
txtstream.WriteLine("   display: inline-block;");
txtstream.WriteLine("   width: 100%;");
txtstream.WriteLine("}");
txtstream.WriteLine("textarea");
txtstream.WriteLine("{");
txtstream.WriteLine("   BORDER-RIGHT: #999999 3px solid;");
txtstream.WriteLine("   PADDING-RIGHT: 3px;");
txtstream.WriteLine("   PADDING-LEFT: 3px;");
txtstream.WriteLine("   FONT-WEIGHT: Normal;");
txtstream.WriteLine("   PADDING-BOTTOM: 3px;");
txtstream.WriteLine("   COLOR: white;");
txtstream.WriteLine("   PADDING-TOP: 3px;");
txtstream.WriteLine("   BORDER-BOTTOM: #999 1px solid;");
txtstream.WriteLine("   BACKGROUND-COLOR: navy;");
txtstream.WriteLine("   FONT-FAMILY: font-family: Cambria, serif;");
txtstream.WriteLine("   FONT-SIZE: 10px;");
txtstream.WriteLine("   text-align: left;");
txtstream.WriteLine("   white-Space: nowrap;");
txtstream.WriteLine("   width: 100%;");
txtstream.WriteLine("}");
txtstream.WriteLine("select");
```

```
txtstream.WriteLine("{");
txtstream.WriteLine("    BORDER-RIGHT: #999999 3px solid;");
txtstream.WriteLine("    PADDING-RIGHT: 6px;");
txtstream.WriteLine("    PADDING-LEFT: 6px;");
txtstream.WriteLine("    FONT-WEIGHT: Normal;");
txtstream.WriteLine("    PADDING-BOTTOM: 6px;");
txtstream.WriteLine("    COLOR: white;");
txtstream.WriteLine("    PADDING-TOP: 6px;");
txtstream.WriteLine("    BORDER-BOTTOM: #999 1px solid;");
txtstream.WriteLine("    BACKGROUND-COLOR: navy;");
txtstream.WriteLine("    FONT-FAMILY: font-family: Cambria, serif;");
txtstream.WriteLine("    FONT-SIZE: 10px;");
txtstream.WriteLine("    text-align: left;");
txtstream.WriteLine("    white-Space: nowrap;");
txtstream.WriteLine("    width: 100%;");
txtstream.WriteLine("}");
txtstream.WriteLine("input");
txtstream.WriteLine("{");
txtstream.WriteLine("    BORDER-RIGHT: #999999 3px solid;");
txtstream.WriteLine("    PADDING-RIGHT: 3px;");
txtstream.WriteLine("    PADDING-LEFT: 3px;");
txtstream.WriteLine("    FONT-WEIGHT: Bold;");
txtstream.WriteLine("    PADDING-BOTTOM: 3px;");
txtstream.WriteLine("    COLOR: white;");
txtstream.WriteLine("    PADDING-TOP: 3px;");
txtstream.WriteLine("    BORDER-BOTTOM: #999 1px solid;");
txtstream.WriteLine("    BACKGROUND-COLOR: navy;");
txtstream.WriteLine("    FONT-FAMILY: font-family: Cambria, serif;");
txtstream.WriteLine("    FONT-SIZE: 12px;");
txtstream.WriteLine("    text-align: left;");
txtstream.WriteLine("    display: table-cell;");
txtstream.WriteLine("    white-Space: nowrap;");
txtstream.WriteLine("    width: 100%;");
```

```
txtstream.WriteLine("}");
txtstream.WriteLine("h1 {");
txtstream.WriteLine("color: antiquewhite;");
txtstream.WriteLine("text-shadow: 1px 1px 1px black;");
txtstream.WriteLine("padding: 3px;");
txtstream.WriteLine("text-align: center;");
txtstream.WriteLine("box-shadow: inset 2px 2px 5px rgba(0,0,0,0.5), inset -2px -2px 5px rgba(255,255,255,0.5)");
txtstream.WriteLine("}");
txtstream.WriteLine("</style>");
```